To Eric & Donna—
I hope you find some
great tips & for
laughter.

Best wishes
Cathy Johnson

WHO MOVED MY TEETH?

PREPARING FOR SELF, LOVED ONES AND CAREGIVING

CATHY SIKORSKI, ESQ.

For all the Caregivers

You are heroes, one and all.

And for John,

Whose support has never wavered,

and who always laughs at my jokes.

Published 2016 by Corner Office Books
Printed in the United States of America

ISBN: 0-9980899-2-3
EAN-13: 978-0-9980899-2-8

Cover art and design by Dwayne Booth

TABLE OF CONTENTS

PART I—START HERE AND NOW

Chapter One   7
    What Should I Have Already Done?

Chapter Two   31
    Medicare, Medicaid and Medigap....Oh My!

Chapter Three   56
    Money

Chapter Four   78
    Are You Socially Secure?

PART II—YOU MIGHT BE A CAREGIVER.......

Chapter Five   87
    Now, Will You Talk to Me?

Chapter Six   100
    How to Ask for Help

Chapter Seven   109
    The Seven Dwarfs of Hidden Symptoms

Chapter Eight   125
    For Heaven's Sake Stop Paying Those Medical Bills!

Chapter Nine   134
    Patience

Chapter Ten   146

    Caring For the Caregiver...Yes, This Means You

Chapter Eleven   156

    How To Make Work, Work For You

Chapter Twelve   161

    Ain't No Shame in Laughing

PART ONE: START HERE AND START NOW

Who Moved My Teeth?

On the seventy-first day of being a caregiver for my 92 year-old Nana, she accused my two-year-old toddler, Rachel of stealing her false teeth. Now, Rachel could have used that commodity as she was a bit deficient in that area. But I was fairly certain Nana was her own culprit.

What could Nana have done with her teeth? The answer was anything. She could have thrown them away. She could have put them in the freezer. She could have put them in the dog's dish. She could have given them to the dog as a gift.

We began the search and rescue. The whole time we were looking for the teeth, Nana was gumming her defense.

"I dmnd't do it."

"I'm sure it was inadvertent, Nana."

"Der mot im my cump."

"What?"

"My cump. Der not dar."

"My cump? My cump? What in the heck is your cump?"

She holds up a pink plastic container in the shape of a large three-dimensional diaphragm holder.

"Oh, your CUP. The cup you clean your teeth in. Okay, good. We know your teeth aren't in there."

"What mid see do mid dem?"

"Who?"

Now this was scary. I totally understood what Nana was saying without her teeth. She wanted to know: "What did she do with them?"

"Her," *Nana said and pointed to the toddler, Rachel.*

Rachel started to cry. She knew she was the accused. I picked Rachel up and tried to console her. I also took the opportunity to sneak a glimpse of her mouth and hands to see if she was hiding the offending teeth. She wasn't and she was offended. She screamed louder.

"Okay, honey. It's okay. Let's put in a movie," *I said.*

"Nana, what do you usually do with your teeth when you go to bed?"

"My cump."

"Right. So, do you remember going to bed last night?"

"Mhm."

"Let's start there."

We went into her bedroom. Surprisingly, everything looked normal. Nothing in any crazy places.

I looked on the dresser. No teeth. I looked on her bedside table. No teeth. I looked on the floor, under the bed, in the closet. She made her bed diligently and immaculately every morning. I saw no teeth chomping to get out through the covers.

Who Moved My Teeth?

I sat on the bed in frustration. I threw my head back on the pillow. The hard, crunchy pillow. Slowly, I lifted the pillow. There they were, as cruddy as that place behind the refrigerator that no one has seen for years.

"Oh my God, Nana, these are disgusting!"

"What?"

She grabbed the teeth from under the pillow and tried to put them in her mouth.

"Noooo!" I practically put her in a chokehold to get the teeth before she could put them in.

"They have to be cleaned. Immediately," I said. For about six months, I thought.

I gingerly placed the teeth between my fingers. I found her cump, but that too needed nuclear blasting. I took the box of Efferdent. The unopened box --had I not been paying attention? --and went downstairs with the offending teeth.

"I'm sorry, Nana but I just have to get these teeth clean first."

"Dat's okay," she said. She trundled off to watch Bert and Ernie with Rachel.

Charlie Chaplin said that life is tragic up close, but from far away it is hysterical.

This introduction to the world of caregiving and ultimately, Elder Law has turned into a 25-year career for me. After caregiving for seven different family members and friends over the last 25 years, I found that the aging community, their children and all caregivers, including myself were learning many things the hard way. This is my small effort to help as many as I can with all that I've learned and continue to learn on our journey together.

Cathy Sikorski

CHAPTER ONE

WHAT SHOULD I HAVE ALREADY DONE?

Here's a list of things you should do if you haven't done them already, either for your loved one that you are/or will be a caregiver for quite soon…OR FOR YOURSELF!

1. **GET A DURABLE POWER OF ATTORNEY….ACTUALLY GET TWO OR THREE!**

   What is a Power of Attorney? This is a critical document that allows someone to take care of your healthcare and business affairs. And everyone in the healthcare and caregiving business will ask you if you have a POA (Power of Attorney).

   A Power of Attorney document comes in a few flavors. There are generally two types of POAs and they need to be Durable, kind of like a good pair of Levi Jeans. Durable means that no matter what happens to you, as a living person, the POA stays in effect. That's a good thing because what would be the whole point of a POA if it doesn't work when you can't. Like my Nana's orthopedic shoes, she was never without them because she needed them for her health. And, during your life, you should never be without your Durable POAs.

A. Durable Health Care Power of Attorney

This document allows a person to make all major and minor healthcare decisions for their loved one. The person who signs the Power of Attorney is giving the *power* to you or someone else to act *as if* you are the signer. So, if your mom signs a Durable POA, and gives the power to you, she has made you her agent. You now have the *power to act as if you are your mom in all health care situations.* If you sign a POA and make your spouse your 'Agent,' your spouse now has the power to act as if he is you in all health care decisions concerning you.

This does not prevent Mom from continuing to make her own decisions about her health care. It does allow the agent, the POA, to make decisions, if necessary. Or, at the very least, as the POA you now have the authority to talk to everyone about your mom's health care.

Does this replace that damned HIPAA form? Yes and yes. There is nothing wrong with you also having your loved one sign a HIPAA form that gives you authority to discuss medical issues, but the Durable Healthcare POA is the best and most powerful document you can have. And it lasts forever, until the person who signed it cancels it in writing. That's why you need 2 or 3 originals. I always gave my clients 3 originals. In case one gets lost, is never returned, or becomes lining for the cat litter box somehow.

An original Durable POA means it has all original signatures and it is signed and witnessed by a Notary Public. So, if you have three original Durable POAs, you will have to sign in all important places 3 times and the Notary will sign each one separately as well.

B. Durable Financial Power of Attorney

This document is different from a Health Care Power of Attorney. The person who signs this type of Durable Power of Attorney is giving the *power* to you or someone else to act *as if* you are that person in all financial situations. So if your mom gives you a Durable Financial POA, you now have the *power to act as if you are your mom in all financial situations.* This too, is a very powerful document. Since the agent is in the shoes of the person who assigned the power. The agent can buy, sell, transfer, pay, not pay and clean out every penny and asset there is. It sounds bad and ominous. And there is no doubt that checks and balances are a good thing when you give a Durable Financial POA to someone. But never underestimate the NEED for this document.

a. Between Spouses

Unless you have a real problem with your spouse, and I'm pretty sure that's a Dr. Phil book, or if your spouse is already suffering from mental incapacity or incapable of making financial decisions, you and your spouse under normal circumstances should give each other Durable Healthcare and Durable Financial POAs.

This is a protection in case anything unplanned would happen to either of you.

You would already have these documents in place to handle any emergency. I'm talking to you. The healthy baby boomer who is reading this, or the Gen-Xer who suddenly realizes their mom and dad are getting older. Hey! We are all getting older! If you are over 18 years old, you should consider Durable POAs for yourself. When my children went to college, I had them sign Durable POAs. As adults living hours away from home, I did not want any nonsense from a hospital or a college administration saying they wouldn't talk to me about my child's condition, be it a health or financial condition.

Fast forward to your own life now. You are 30-something or 40-something. You have kids, a nice house, a couple of cars. You have an accident. You are disabled. You're in a coma. Your husband can't sell the house, car, or shares in Microsoft, because they belong to you. The hospital wants to put a shunt in your brain to stop the bleeding but no one has the authority to say "yay" or "nay." That's why everyone needs Durable POAs at every stage of their adult life. Not when you're 85 years old and you think, "hey, something might happen to me."

DO IT NOW, DO IT NOW, DO IT NOW.

No one even needs to know you have these documents. You can go to your local wonderful attorney, get the paperwork done, put it in your fireproof box in the basement, and when someone needs to find your important papers....Voila!! There it is. Just make sure someone knows you have important papers and where they are located.

b.   A Word on Durable POAs

Besides being the most important document you may not have yet and need to get, POA's can also be like a Chinese menu. Any lawyer worth her salt will take you through a process where you need to decide exactly *how much* power you want to bestow. In Pennsylvania, for example, where I reside, there are very strict rules about things like how much money can the POA give as a gift and to whom. So please, find a lawyer. Ask your friends, neighbors, someone you know who has dealt with issues like this. Research lawyers, but find one, and get your affairs in order. It's that important, because if you need this and you don't have it, this is what happens next................

c.   Whom Do I Choose to be my POA?

This question is complicated. Usually, if you are healthy and happy as a couple, you would choose each other as your primary POA. You should always have an alternate POA in case something happens to both of you simultaneously.

If your spouse is unable to be your POA, or you don't have a spouse, you need to choose a person you can trust completely. This person will have power over your money and your health. You need to choose wisely.

Normally, it would be best to choose a daughter or son or other relative who lives close by. Making these decisions, especially with hospitals and doctors usually needs a person who is available to go to those places or meet with those healthcare professionals.

When deciding who to choose as your POA ask yourself some questions:

1. Do I trust this person completely with my money and/or my health?
2. Will they be available to make decisions at a moment's notice?
3. Are they capable of making these decisions?
4. Does this person know how to find and ask for help for me?
5. Do I want to put all the financial or health care power with one person, or do I want to give joint or several powers?

   Caution: It can be challenging to have joint POAs because if they disagree, there is no one to 'break the tie.' You can have 'either or' POA's. So that if you name your son and daughter as joint POA's, your son and daughter can make decisions jointly or by themselves (severally). Note that they need to be able to work together for the several powers as they can make decisions without the other's input. If you don't see that happening, then choose one decider and an alternate.

I DON'T HAVE A POA AND CAN'T GET ONE, NOW WHAT DO I DO?

The reason you need this POA is because someone needs your help and they are incapacitated. Or the reason you need this POA is that you need help because you are temporarily or permanently incapacitated. The reason you don't have one is because someone didn't know they needed to get their affairs in order. This is not unusual or judgmental. Lots and lots of people don't know they need POAs until it's too late. Not only old, sick people are uninformed, but young, healthy people think they are infallible. It's understandable. Many of us don't ever see a lawyer in our lifetime. Why would you? If you're not suing your neighbor over the fence he built on your property, or you are happy with the car insurance settlement you got from Allstate, you wouldn't bother with a lawyer.

However, when you need a lawyer's help, it's often because you needed it before that bad thing happened. For instance, your widowed uncle was recently diagnosed with Alzheimer's Disease, or you had an accident that temporarily left you unable to handle your affairs, or your dad went into a nursing home and your mom has never written a check because dad handled all their business.

Now you need a Healthcare POA for dad in that nursing home, a Durable Financial POA for dad and mom as you take over their bills, taxes, and investments. And you don't have one.

At this point, you need "A Decider." What can you do if you or your loved is not mentally capable of understanding or signing legal documents?

It's a fixable problem. But it's complicated and expensive. So very much more expensive than having spent the time and money to get this done when everyone was healthy and happy.

You need to hire a lawyer, right now. They will take you through the guardianship process. Someone-- hopefully you--will be appointed guardian of Dad and perhaps Mom if she is not mentally competent to handle her affairs as well. If Mom is still competent, yay!!! You can take Mom to an attorney and have her complete her Durable Healthcare and Durable Financial POAs. But you still need a Guardianship for Dad if he is and will remain mentally incompetent.

NO ONE CAN SIGN A POWER OF ATTORNEY GIVING AUTHORITY TO AN AGENT IF THE SIGNER IS MENTALLY INCOMPETENT AND HAS NO UNDERSTANDING OF WHAT THEY ARE SIGNING.

Since every POA must be notarized, a Notary Public should not be allowing incompetent people to sign legal documents of any kind.

So, now what?

Now you have to go to court and get a Guardianship. With the help of your lawyer, you will appear before a judge. You will have petitioned for Guardianship based on testimony, either in person or if your state allows it, by deposition of a licensed physician who must testify that your loved one is incompetent.

Once you have the Guardianship in place, your state will likely have filing requirements for you to keep the Court abreast of how you are spending the assets. It's a huge pain in the you-know-what.

Who Moved My Teeth?

I am not advocating that you don't keep very good records of taking care of your loved ones. Keep all your receipts, make Excel Spreadsheets, keep track of your time spent, so that you have that information if any old busy-body Ms. Gulch tries to question your motives, hard work or good intentions. But it's much easier to be a good record keeper and be able to show your mom, your sister, your brother-in-law everything you've done, rather than being subject to the whims of the court and having to keep an attorney on retainer to do those filings.

What I am saying is that a lengthy, expensive and on-going court intervention is not make your life easier with your loved ones in the long run.

Aside: At really boring cocktail parties, when the talk turns from aches and pains to elder law matters, I often hear, "Oh I don't need a POA, I'm my Mom's executor, so I have that covered.

No, no, no, no, no, no, no.

If you are your mother's executor, that means that when your mother dies, her Last Will and Testament which she has signed, appoints you the executor of her estate and you are now responsible to take care of all the estate matters that happen after her death.

POA's are for living people. Wills are for dead people. That's it.

So here's my poem. Memorize it and pass it on at all those boring cocktail parties.

POA alive today,
Once you pass away,
Only an Executor can play.

2. MAKE SURE YOUR WILL IS IN ORDER

Lots of great couples get their act together when they have those beautiful little babies come into their lives. They get their behinds to a lawyer's office and make out a will. Usually after fighting for days, weeks or months over whose mom would be the better guardian of their precious offspring if the plane goes down.

That young couple finally decides to pick one mom over the other (may she never find out) and also choose a competent brother-in-law who is in banking or at least balances his checkbook to take care of the finances when they are gone. They sigh a big huge 'whew' of relief and then let it sit for 25 or 30 or even 40 years.

You go into mom and dad's safe deposit box in the bank or fireproof box in the basement, and there it is, the will they made before you got married and had your 2.5 children and had the same fight with your husband as to whose mom would be the best guardian for your children.

I've seen this more times than I can count.

You don't have to be a nosy so-and-so. Just ask your parents, or yourself, for that matter, when was the last time you updated or even looked at your will. Do the decisions you made 5, 7, 10, 15 or in your parents' case 40 years ago, make any sense today? If not, when you go to that lawyer for your new POA's have her update your will as well.

She will ask you to think about who you want to be in charge of your children now and your finances. And when you die, how do you want your estate distributed if you experience what lawyers so lovingly refer to as "the holocaust scenario." That's where you and all your immediate loved ones are wiped out by a volcano, or other catastrophic event. I know it's a bit scary and gruesome, but you think about it for a couple of days, sign some papers, put them in that fireproof box (in case of volcano) and forget about it. You've done it before, perhaps, and your parents have probably done it too! So get to it.

Now as to your parents, elders, or any others for whom you may be a caregiver for, get them to that lawyer's office as well. Get things set up so that they have that precious POA and an updated will with an Executor, and their final wishes for children, grandchildren, charities and Grandma's wedding ring and Grandpa's golf clubs are taken care of.

Aside: When you take your parents to the lawyer's office, you do not go in there with them until your presence is requested. Or, in the alternative, you can initially explain why you are there and then expect to be asked to leave the office for a private conversation. This is to assure the lawyer that your mom/or dad are making their own decisions. If your parents are already struggling with dementia or Alzheimer's or any issue that would cause mental incompetence, then you and your parents don't belong in that lawyer's office for them to make independent decisions. If your parents can't sign legal documents, they won't be allowed to. Don't be offended when the lawyer says, "I would like to speak to your mom and/or dad without you in the office." This is for your protection, your parent's protection and it is a sign that the lawyer is doing a good job.

Wills can be complicated but not always. Frankly, wills get more complicated when you have more assets. Assets include real estate, bank accounts, investment accounts, savings accounts, trusts, savings bonds, furniture, jewelry and just general stuff. Depending on how complicated your assets are, your lawyer may suggest trying to use trusts to avoid taxes,

17

avoid your sister-in-law from getting anything, or to make sure your grandchildren get a piece of the pie. If you have minor aged children you will have a trust provision in your will to provide a guardian and trustee for your children. But beware, that is not the kind of trust that is used for investment and tax purposes.

The other way wills can get complicated is if you have a family member who has special needs. If you have a child, brother, sister, aunt, uncle, cousin, or grandchild who has mental health issues or physical health issues they will require a Special Needs Trust. In that case, a will can be a more complex document. These are very important documents used to protect assets for loved ones with Special Needs. If you have someone in your family with Special Needs and have not researched this, please do so as soon as possible. This type of document is drafted by attorneys who work in the field of Estates and Trusts. Find a lawyer who has done this type of work and consult with them. Special Needs Trusts are necessary to provide support for your disabled loved ones and also allow them to retain their disability benefits. Many people have generously left money to a disabled sibling or grandchild, only to put that disabled person in financial jeopardy because there was no Special Needs Trust in place. If the Special Needs Trust is not created in a timely manner, benefits that would continue to go to the disabled person can be terminated.

But over and above all of that, a will can be a pretty straightforward document. Any good lawyer will be able to meet the needs of young couples, couples with teens, and moms and dads with grown children and kids of their own.

ASIDE: Just a word on Trusts. This has become a buzzword that appears as attractive as Ginger on Gilligan's Island, but it can be just smoke and mirrors like Mrs. Thurston Howell III. Trusts are always used when you are setting up a way for your minor children to receive the assets of your estate over their lifetime. This is because minor children cannot inherit outright. The law requires a trustee, so that someone can be responsible for a minor child's assets until they reach the age of majority.

But then there are Living Trusts. This is the buzzword that makes everyone think they have found the motherlode for keeping Uncle Sam out of your business and keeping the tax man away. Do your homework. A Living Trust, can be revocable or irrevocable. It is made during your lifetime, where you, the grantor (or creator of the trust) will put your assets in a trust which are then distributed after your death to your beneficiaries.

The big advantage to the Living Trust is touted as 'these assets do not have to go through probate which can be expensive and take time.' This may be true but it may not be true and it may not be an advantage.

Paying for probate in our state of Pennsylvania, is a few hundred dollars at best. So what if you avoid probate? Would you rather pay thousands now for document preparation of a Living Trust or a few hundred out of your estate after you've passed away? Those probate costs are deductible from inheritance tax, but the thousands you spent on that Living Trust....not deductible. Oh, and by the way, you're probably still going to pay some tax..

The other 'selling' point is that since your estate is not on record with the court no one can see what you left your family. Okay, that's true. But really, who do you think is going to the courthouse after you've died to see what you left to your kids and the local firehouse? Unless you're George Clooney, no one cares. But if you care so much that you will spend an extra few thousand dollars of your hard-earned money for that level of privacy after you're dead, well, have at it. But please do your homework. At the end of this is a list of questions to ask when someone tells you you need a living trust.

There are certainly times when a living trust is an important document. And again, a good trusts and estate lawyer will know if you are a candidate for such a thing. However, I have seen many a client come to me with a "living trust" created by a financial planner, which turned out to be a beautiful plastic binder filled with paper that was useless and cost the client thousands of dollars. If you are going to look into a living trust, consult an attorney, not a financial planner. Or at the very least, have your financial planner talk to your lawyer. Because the burning question is:" How is this trust funded?" I have seen trusts that were 'created' with not a thing put in them. If you don't put anything in the trust, all you have is paper, not a trust.

Okay these are the important trust questions:

1. *Why do I need a living trust?*

2. *How much does probate cost that I am 'avoiding' and what does that actually mean? Does it mean that I just do not have to file papers in court?*

3. *How does a living trust avoid taxes? Won't I still have to pay inheritance tax? What tax exactly does it avoid?*

4. *How are you going to fund the trust?*

5. *What assets of mine will go into the trust and what can I do or not do with those assets once they are in the trust?*

6. *How does that trust co-ordinate with Medicaid? How much does it affect the look back period for assets I have already gifted?*

7. *How much is this going to cost me and how much will my estate save by entering into this trust situation?*

If you ask these question, and you don't get straight up answers that satisfy you, move on. It's very possible that a trust is for you, but it's also very possible that it's a red herring and is so NOT for you.

3. THE LIVING WILL OR AS COMPLICATED PEOPLE LIKE TO CALL IT, AN ADVANCED DIRECTIVE.

This is the document that everyone is afraid of. Yes, it's the Karen Ann Quinlan/Terry Schiavo document. It's where you put in writing what you want to happen *if you are in a permanent vegetative state.*

Let me say that again: *if you are in a permanent vegetative state.*

Don't be sending yourself or anyone else you know into a tizzy thinking that if you go in for an appendectomy that you're going to be put on life support. Sure, anything can happen, but the whole point of an Advanced Directive is that you have had the opportunity to think about what you would like to have done in the direst of circumstances.

An Advanced Directive tells the whole world that you have thought about a situation where it is ever so likely that you will not be resuscitated. So in those

21

circumstances, what kind of extraordinary care do you want and what kind of organ donorship are you interested in. These documents are usually very easy to understand and easy to fill out.

But here's the caveat: In Pennsylvania, for example, these documents are like stop signs in Rome, Italy. They are only a suggestion. If medical professionals do not honor your wishes, either because they were not aware of them or because, well they just didn't, you have no recourse. So just be prepared that these documents, although helpful, are not written in stone. The good news is, if you take the time to fill out one of these forms, you have, at the very least given your family a very good, very black and white way of letting them know what your wishes truly are. So I'm in favor of a Living Will or an Advanced Directive. Just so you know that it's like the duct tape in your toolbox, useful but not critical.

A. A DNR

Yes, you will have to become fluent in acronyms. A DNR can be a part of an Advanced Directive or it can be separate. But it's pretty darn important. Probably more so than the entire rest of the Advanced Directive.

DNR means DO NOT RESUSCITATE.

So if you, or as Healthcare POA for your loved one, have come to the conclusion that you do not wish to be resuscitated should you go into heart failure or any other immediate life threatening failure, you can sign a DNR. By signing a DNR, you are asking the medical team, the hospice team, or the nursing home team to fail to take heroic measures to resuscitate you. This is truly not to be taken lightly. Generally, a DNR is not signed until you or your loved one has come to a place in their health that many more days of poking and prodding is just not in the cards physically, emotionally, psychologically, and everyone has agreed that it would be best for nature to take its course.

Now as you can imagine, a DNR can cause conflict and problems. Many a family member is not ready to make final and painful decisions like this. An advance decision by you is the best, but truthfully, it usually falls to the Healthcare POA. I myself, had to make this decision as a caregiver more than once. It's not easy, but when you need to stop the insanity, you will be glad you have such a document available to you. And, truth be told, the medical community does appreciate it when the decision is made, and it's the right decision. No one said this was easy. Just putting the right tools in the tool box can always make it better.

4. LONG TERM CARE INSURANCE

You are going to hear lots of pros and cons about Long Term Care Insurance. Long Term Care Insurance is a product that you purchase to defray the cost of a nursing home. It is sometimes called Nursing Home Insurance, not by any insurance people, because then they couldn't come up with ways to convince you to buy this fancy named product. But I'm going to try. I don't sell Long Term Care Insurance. I do have Long Term Care Insurance and I've had it with my husband for many years. We first bought Long Term Care Insurance when it was offered as an optional benefit at work. When they privatized it, and offered it only directly to us, we still chose to keep it. Here is the reason why.

Nursing home admissions and paying for care in a nursing home is a very expensive and very complicated process. There should be entire books about this topic alone. There are reams and reams of laws in every state and in the Federal Government on issues surrounding nursing home admissions and costs.

Here are some simplified highlights of the nursing home process and how and why Long Term Care Insurance can be a critical planning tool for your future.

Two scenarios may best describe how Long Term Care Insurance works:

A. A Married Couple

> Let's call them Bob and Carol. They have been happily married for 50 years. They are now 86 and 83. Bob suffers a terrible stroke and is admitted to a nursing home for 'rehab.' This is where you go from the requisite 3 day stay in a hospital to a nursing

home facility that also qualifies as a rehabilitation center.

Bob does well in rehab. But not well enough. Carol, at 83 years old, is not capable of taking care of Bob at home without significant assistance.

Carol has a few choices here:

1.) She can keep Bob at the rehabilitation center if they are also a high end assisted living facility or a nursing home.

2.) She can research a new facility that is either high end assisted living or nursing home care, depending on what Bob's needs are determined to be.

3.) She can take Bob home and hire a Home Health Agency to come every day and help with bathing, dressing and feeding Bob, if necessary. Keep in mind that because Carol took Bob home she is now ineligible for the rest of the 100 days that Medicare would have paid for him to be in a nursing home facility.

Carol decides to bring Bob home and hire an agency. This goes well for about 2 weeks when Alice, their daughter, gets tired of coming over

25

every night to help with her dad because the caregiver has gone home for the day.

The average cost of a nursing home in Carol's state is $10,000 per month (yes, that's 10 with 3 zeros after it and it is per month). Because Carol and Bob have built a nice retirement life for themselves, Carol is expected to pay the full cost of the nursing home until she only has $2,400 left in savings and about $120,000 in assets. Carol is expected to live off of that for the rest of her life. She can keep her own Social Security and any pensions or annuities in her own name (and this may or may not be true in every state). But since Carol was a stay-at-home mom and right after that became a caregiver for her mother, she never returned to the work force nor created a retirement savings plan for herself.

Carol can keep her house and her car and all her personal belongings in her home. Bob was the 'breadwinner' and all of their retirement funds are in Bob's name, e.g. Bob's 401K, Bob's stock options, Bob's pension and profit sharing, Bob's larger Social Security check. So as it stands right now, Bob is expected to use all of that money to pay for his care. This leaves Carol looking at leaving behind her current lifestyle completely. She cannot afford to pay the mortgage and taxes on her home. She cannot pay for any upkeep and with her paltry Social Security, the cost of groceries, gas, and her own doctor appointments is now out of reach for her.

Carol knows that Bob bought some kind of nursing home insurance somewhere in the past, but has to go through all their important papers to find the information. She calls her daughter, Alice to come help with the search.

Alice and Carol find the policy and call the Insurance Company. They are sent documents for a claim which includes documents that must go to Bob's physician to confirm his nursing home eligibility. For this, the doctor's office charges $25.00.

With this nursing home insurance, Carol can find a good Elder Law attorney and legally work out a system where she can use their excess funds to set up an annuity for her and transfer funds to her name in legitimate, legal ways while the Long Term Care Insurance defrays the cost of Bob's nursing home care.

This is an over-simplification of a convoluted system which often results in many elders, especially women who have forgone the opportunities to create their own retirement, ending up destitute, eating cat food and yes, homeless.

That's why I'm an advocate of Long Term Care Insurance.

There are many products out there. You need to find an Elder Law attorney to work with your financial person to make sure you purchase a product that works for you. This is *not* a one-size-fits-all arena. You have to be diligent and look at your personal financial situation to see how Long Term Care Insurance fits into your life. But if you are in your 40's or 50's or even 60's you are young by Long

Term Care Insurance standards and you can find a policy that will save you much grief and money in the future if you need it.

Yes, it's like any other insurance, if you don't use it you paid for it anyway. There are even exceptions as some policies may act as life insurance as well. Regardless of what you choose, if you can fit this type of product into your planning and budget, you may be very grateful. Quite frankly, do you really want to be looking homelessness in the face at 83 years old?

>B. A Single Person----a legacy----also you may get to pick a better nursing home.

>The rules are a bit different if you are a single person. On the one hand, you do not have to worry about leaving a spouse out in the world with no money and no housing. On the other hand, if you have any kind of investments, savings, retirement funds built up, you probably would like a little bit of a say as to where that money would go in your old age or at your death.

>The reason this becomes important, as a single person, is that you may be choosing a retirement lifestyle that places you in a community where they have what is known as "step-down" arrangements.

>There's a beautiful community in my area. It was once a huge and prosperous horse farm. It is now a community of apartments for Senior Living. It has a theater, restaurants, a bowling alley, art studios, woodworking studios,

swimming pools, gymnasiums, walking trails, and every amenity you would care to have.

There is also has a rehabilitation center, assisted living center and a nursing home center as part of the whole community.

If you choose to live your golden years here, you will be covered for every eventuality. And it's expensive.

However, if you do end up needing assistance and eventual nursing home care, Long Term Care Insurance can do several things to make this fancy pants journey that you have earned and created even better.

You will be able to have your Long Term Care Insurance Policy defray the cost of assisted care or nursing care while you may be able to place some of your assets in the hands of those you wish to honor with your legacy.

So if you want your niece to have the Interior Design business she always dreamed of, you may now have a chance to gift those funds to her. If you wish to support the Animal Rescue League who so greatly gave you the best Yellow Labrador Retrievers who ever graced your back yard, now is the time to give to charity.

And even if you just want to stay in the assisted living facility, which is not and seems like it will never be covered by Medicaid, your Long Term Care Insurance will give you the extra funds to extend your time at a place *you* have chosen.

So, see? You need to do some homework on this type of insurance product. You need to see if it fits in your budget in any way. You need to get it if you can, unless the rules somehow change and we are all not expected to make ourselves poor at the prospect of our spouse going into a nursing home. And I don't see that changing anytime soon.

Now you know what you should have done or should be doing, so if you do lose your teeth or someone else's teeth, you know to be prepared and how to find your cump!

CHAPTER TWO

MEDICARE, MEDIGAP AND MEDICAID.....OH MY!

The difference between Medicare, Medigap and Medicaid. Does somebody keep making spelling mistakes or are they really different?

I had quickly navigated the murky waters of HIPAA and POAs to get medical providers to talk to me for my brother-in-law's care. And then he passed away and I became his Executrix. And it began all over again.

Hello, Medicare? I've now sent you a request for permission to speak to me as Executrix of my brother-in-law's estate with all the supporting documents. I've waited the requisite 50 days for you to process it, and now I have finally received a letter saying you will talk to me. Yay.

Medicare Person: What can I help you with today?

Me: I'm trying to find out when a claim I have submitted will be paid?

Medicare Person: Why did you submit the claim Ma'am?

Me: Because the provider refused to submit it. They provide drugs and drug paraphernalia to the nursing home where my brother-in-law was residing at the time. They insist that they can only bill for the drugs to Part D Medicare and they have no authority to submit for the other items like IV poles, IV flushes and anything needed to actually administer the drugs.

Medicare Person (the THIRD Medicare person who speaks to me, because the first two couldn't find the other conversations I've had and insisted that no such conversations took place). Yes, I've found the conversations you've had on April 4th, 11th, and 22nd.

Me: The last person I spoke with who connected me to you said she couldn't find those conversations.

Medicare Person: Well, you're both right. She can't see these conversations, she's in a different department.

Me: So, she couldn't transfer me to you without wasting 30 minutes of my time and me insisting I speak to this department?

Medicare Person: I apologize for that Ma'am.

Me being Silent.

Medicare Person: Well, Ma'am I can't find your claim. it takes 50 days to process.

Who Moved My Teeth?

Me: I filed that claim 120 days ago, and when your Medicare person CALLED ME ON APRIL 22 while I was standing in the middle of Times Square, and I popped into the closest restaurant and ordered a $12 glass of wine while on hold with your person, she told me that she was looking at my claim. I was told the claim was paid to the nursing home. Then Medicare sent me the wrong Medicare notices so I could not prove to the nursing home, they owed the provider.

Medicare Person: I can't find that claim Ma'am. And so the only thing I can do is request a review.

Me: Okay.

Medicare Person: I'm not allowed to request a review until 150 days has passed and it's only been 120 since you filed the claim. A denial can take up to 150 days to process.

A missing claim is like a missing person. Maybe they went missing on their own. Maybe they are just at a friend's house and forgot to tell you. Maybe they will use a credit card and then we can trace where they are and stop all this nonsense. But instead of waiting 48 hours, you have to wait 150 days. Imagine telling any person you've ever worked with that it will take 150 days to look at a piece of paper you sent them.

Medicare Person: I know this is complicated and confusing Ma'am.

Me: I understand perfectly, everything you've told me. It's not complicated or confusing to me, it's just crazy! (Yep, I really did say that).

Medicare Person: Well, I know it seems complex, but we train for WEEKS to process this, so it would be harder for you to understand.

WEEKS? WEEKS? I've been dealing with Medicare for 25 years. And in all your weeks of training, the best you guys have ever given me is ridiculous, arbitrary waiting periods to process claims, a myriad of departments who don't speak to each other, wrong information that has cost me precious time, and heartburn without the doughnut, wine or deep-fried food I deserve to go with it.

So glad your weeks of training have made you an expert.

I didn't say any of that, I just got out my corkscrew and toasted the Universe for the never-ending supply of blog posts!

MEDICARE

Medicare is a health insurance plan for people 65 years of age and older. The only thing you need to do to qualify for Medicare is to reach the magical age of 65.

Once you do reach that magical age of 65 years, you must apply for Medicare as your medical health insurance. You apply for Medicare on line at www.medicare.gov or you can make an appointment at your local Social Security Office. I say must, however, like every other government game, this one has its chutes and ladders.

You should apply for Medicare Parts A and B (see description below) at age 65. You can begin the process three months before your 65th birthday. If you are retired, unemployed or disabled (which has other chutes and ladders in this story), you should do this without fail.

If you are still working and covered by your employer's insurance, you have to consult with your Human Resources Department about how your health insurance coordinates with Medicare. This is very important. If your employer requires you to sign up for Medicare, Medicare becomes primary. This means Medicare pays your medical bills first, and your employee health insurance pays the balances. You still must sign up for Parts A and B by age 65.

If your employer does not require you to sign up for Medicare, Medicare becomes secondary. This means your employee health insurance pays your medical bills first, and then Medicare kicks in some or all of the balances, if you choose to purchase Medicare. You also have the option of delaying your Medicare sign up, until you quit working, retire, or lose your job.

This, however, is shark infested waters. Cue the music from *Jaws*.

It is often better to sign up for Medicare at age 65, for most of us. Part A is no cost to participants. But there is a monthly fee for Medicare Part B. The scary part is described below.

Currently the fee for Part B is $121.80 per month (there are higher rates for high-income participants). This fee is taken directly out of your Social Security check before you even see it.

However, if you don't sign up for Medicare Part B when you qualify, at age 65, there can be a penalty forever. The penalty is calculated by the number of months you basically were not on the insurance starting at age 65. So if you retired at age 70, and you didn't sign up for Part B at age 65, there can be an additional fee added on to that $121.80 every single month as a penalty for not signing up when you could. The exception to that rule (see now you're going through the chute) is if you were covered by your employer's health insurance during that period of time. But your employer's insurance has to meet certain requirements.

If your employer's insurance is so good that you don't need and don't buy a Medicare Part B, you may be eligible to wait to purchase Part B until you are no longer employed. This can be a good thing, as you aren't paying the Part B premium and you delay the Open Enrollment period so that no medical pre-existing conditions can be used against you to increase premiums on a Medigap policy or deny you a Medigap policy altogether. This is so time sensitive that it is scary. If you take the Part B, while you are employed and don't purchase a Medigap policy, because you don't need one, you lose that Open Enrollment. The reason Open Enrollment is so important is that if you have any pre-existing medical conditions, it doesn't matter, Medigap companies must take you as an insured. There are exceptions to this rule and the medicare.gov website has good clear FAQs about this under the topic "When can I buy Medigap? So check with Social Security and check with your employer *before* you turn age 65.

To add insult to injury, now that most of us are not eligible for full retirement benefits until age 66 or older, we will not be receiving a Social Security check until after we turn 65 years old. So the Social Security Administration can't take the Medicare premium out of your Social Security check. You have to pay the bill until you start receiving a Social Security check. When you finally sign up for Social Security at age 66 or older (not Medicare, that's at age 65) the premium for your Medicare will be deducted from your Social Security check.

I know…………..WHAT?

All that being said, look into signing up for Parts A and B before you turn age 65. If you're working and have health insurance at work, talk to Human Resources AND Social Security before you turn 65 to find out what you must, should and can do to get the most for your money and not suffer any penalties in the future.

Medicare is trickier than Dungeons and Dragons. I don't care what aspect of it you are dealing with. As soon as you think you have climbed the ladder of questions, concerns, advice and decisions, you fall down the chute of exceptions, omissions, exclusions and definitions.

It is pointless for me to re-invent the wheel here as there are pages and pages of explanations about Medicare at their website: www.medicare.gov

I, for one, am astounded as to how anyone thinks people who haven't dealt with insurance, nursing homes, hospital administration, pharmacy providers, durable medical equipment providers, etc., would think that the convoluted Medicare rules and regulations would be easy to understand or navigate.

But I will say, the website is pretty darn good. It's written in plain English and it is designed to answer common questions. If you don't know the common questions, I'm going to give you some here. You can navigate the website and get your questions answered. And, as a big bonus, there is a box called "Find Someone to Talk To" where you put in your state and a list of agencies will appear who are designed to help you with this process.

It is an excellent website. Go over there and scroll around. Read everything you can. Read about each part of Medicare, Part A, Part B, Part C and Part D. My brief explanations will give you a starting point, but there is no substitute for reading all you can on the website.

What is Medicare Part A?

Medicare Part A (hospitalization) pays for:

1. Hospital Bills (after the deductible which changes every year)

2. SOME Nursing home costs (which are referred to as SNF or "snif" meaning Skilled Nursing Facility)

   a. These costs are paid for 100 days.

   b. These costs are only paid after a 3 day ADMITTED stay into the hospital, when you are released on the 4th day or thereafter to a SNF.

   c. You can leave the SNF and come back within 30 days if you need skilled nursing, without a return to the hospital for 3 days.

   d. Days 1-20 are free, after that days 21-100 you must pay a co-pay which is $161 per day right now, but changes every year. And by changes, I mean it goes up, it never goes down.

   e. You only re-start the 100 days of payment for skilled nursing if you have had no skilled nursing for a 60 day period after that first admission.

3. Hospice

4. Home health services (under certain restrictions)

WHAT IS MEDICARE PART B?

Part B pays for: (medical)

1. Some Doctor's Services

2. Outpatient Care

3. Medical Supplies

4. Preventative Health Care Services

WHAT IS MEDICARE PART C?

Medicare Part C :

This is the plan that is commonly called the Medicare Advantage Plans. These are the HMO's (Health Maintenance Organizations), the PPO's (Preferred Provider Organizations) PFFS (Private Fee For Service Organizations) and SNP (Special Needs Plans)

All of these Medicare Part C Plans take you out of Original Medicare and put you in a Plan where choice of doctor, medical provider, and services are subject to the rules these Plans have created.

Choosing a Medicare Part C Plan or as it's known a Medicare Advantage Plan puts you in the hands of the Plan rules and regulations you are choosing.

So choose wisely. Make sure you read all the Plan has to offer. Make certain you are happy with your choice of doctors, hospitals, nursing homes or home health aides if these are services that you use regularly.

Don't be fooled by the term Medicare Advantage, it may or may not be to your Advantage. It may be much more beneficial for you to choose Original Medicare and then purchase a Medigap policy to cover any costs that Medicare does not pay, or a Part C Plan may serve your needs best. You must also continue to be aware of health underwriting and pre-existing conditions. You can't switch between Original Medicare and Medicare Advantage willy-nilly. You can only 'safely' do it during Fall Open Enrollment and other rare exceptions. And even Fall Open Enrollment does not guarantee protection from pre-existing conditions.

Yes, we have to talk about Medigap Policies. Let's finish our alphabet soup of Medicare and then we will have a chat about Medigap.

WHAT IS MEDICARE PART D?

Medicare Part D pays for:

1. Prescription Drug Plans.

   Now this looks like it might be self-explanatory. That would be too simple.

   Yes, this is the Plan where you choose a prescription plan. Seems easy. I need a plan to pay for my prescriptions. Then Medicare Part D sends you a book, not even a booklet, a book with the choices of prescription plans in it. It has charts and graphs and numbers.

   And that's only the choice of drug plans.

   Then you have to open up the formulary and see if the drugs you take are in there and which tier they are on and then see how Prescription Drug Company 1, 2, 3, 7, 14, or 22 pays for your drugs.

When I was planning for my brother-in-law, he was taking at least 15 different drugs every single day. I had to wade through the formulary to make sure his drugs were covered. I also wanted to see the cost of said drugs to make sure that joining a Medicare Plan C which included prescriptions, might be a better cost than Original Medicare, Medigap and Medicare Plan D.

I just went to the website, www.medicare.gov and typed in my zip code, prescriptions, dosages and chosen pharmacies. Now the good news is they have this wonderful thing where you can type in all your meds, choose a pharmacy or two in your area, and then it spits out the drug plans and tells you if your drugs are covered as well as the cost of the plan.

The bad news is it came up with 47 plans from which to choose.

This is not for the faint of heart.

If this is too much for you, get someone to help you. There are Senior agencies, AARP agencies and help with Medicare agencies all over the place. They are even listed in that groovy box I told you about that says, "Find Someone to Talk To," right on the Medicare sight which gives you contact information for many of these places where you can get help.

Yes, you should investigate help for Seniors in your area. Many Senior centers, hospitals, and even some churches with senior groups have programs where experts come in and discuss with you how to navigate the Medicare System and make informed choices about your insurance.

MEDIGAP POLICIES

Medigap Policies are insurance policies that pay the gap in charges from the amounts that Medicare does not pay. Medicare does not pay everything 100%. You purchase a Medigap Policy with your own money in order to have these additional benefits over and above Original Medicare. Your Medigap policy could be from Aetna, United Healthcare, AARP, or a myriad of other insurance companies that sell Medigap Policies. So when you go to the doctor or hospital and you have a coinsurance and a deductible that you have to meet every year, your Medigap policy might pay all of that coinsurance and all or some of that deductible. Because these costs can add up, many people have found that the cost of a Medigap policy is well worth it.

If you have a Medicare Part C Plan, you may have, as part of that HMO, PPO, or any other Part C plan, built-in benefits that reduce or eliminate deductibles and copays. But you cannot have a Medigap Policy with your Medicare Part C. It's not allowed. So again, choose wisely, get help and remember every year during enrollment from about October 15th to about December 5th you can change your plans completely.

For example: You go to Dr. Brown's office for a pain in the neck (no not your husband). The person at the front desk takes your Medicare card and your Medigap Policy card. You might have a copay of $10 and that might be the end of it. You might have an additional bill to meet your deductible for the year. After you've satisfied the deductible, your Medigap policy will likely cover everything outside your copays for the rest of the year.

Without that Medigap policy, you will likely get a bill from Dr. Brown every time you go see him. And you will get a balance bill for every time you go to the hospital, or any other doctor. The Medigap policy, especially a good one, will take care of most of those expenses not covered by Medicare. If you go to the doctor, or you are a caregiver for someone who goes to the doctor, it's wise to have a Medigap policy. But remember, this is only for people who have chosen Medicare and Medigap, these rules don't necessarily apply if you have a Part C/Medicare Advantage Plan.

The charts below are from the Medicare website. They indicate what type of coverage you can purchase. The Medigap Plans A through N are named that from every Medigap provider. These are the benefits those various plans will provide. The cost depends on the company you choose. That information comes to you during open enrollment. If you haven't become adept at this, as I said, many Senior Centers offer advice during open enrollment for you to make good decisions.

The chart below shows basic information about the different benefits Medigap policies cover.

Medigap Benefits	Medigap Plans									
	A	B	C	D	F	G	K	L	M	N
Part A coinsurance and hospital costs up to an additional 365 days after Medicare benefits are used up	Yes	Yes	Yes	Yes	Yes	Yes	Yes	Yes	Yes	Yes
Part B coinsurance or copayment	Yes	Yes	Yes	Yes	Yes	Yes	50%	75%	Yes	Yes***
Blood (first 3 pints)	Yes	Yes	Yes	Yes	Yes	Yes	50%	75%	Yes	Yes
Part A hospice care coinsurance or copayment	Yes	Yes	Yes	Yes	Yes	Yes	50%	75%	Yes	Yes
Skilled nursing facility care coinsurance	No	No	Yes	Yes	Yes	Yes	50%	75%	Yes	Yes
Part A deductible	No	Yes	Yes	Yes	Yes	Yes	50%	75%	50%	Yes
Part B deductible	No	No	Yes	No	Yes	No	No	No	No	No
Part B excess charge	No	No	No	No	Yes	Yes	No	No	No	No
Foreign travel exchange (up to plan limits)	No	No	80%	80%	80%	80%	No	No	80%	80%
Out-of-pocket limit**	N/A	N/A	N/A	N/A	N/A	N/A	$4,960	$2,480	N/A	N/A

Compare Medigap plans side-by-side

Yes = the plan covers 100% of this benefit

No = the policy doesn't cover that benefit

% = the plan covers that percentage of this benefit

N/A = not applicable

* Plan F also offers a high-deductible plan. If you choose this option, this means you must pay for Medicare-covered costs up to the deductible amount of $2,180 in 2016 before your Medigap plan pays anything.

** After you meet your out-of-pocket yearly limit and your yearly Part B deductible, the Medigap plan pays 100% of covered services for the rest of the calendar year.

*** Plan N pays 100% of the Part B coinsurance, except for a copayment of up to $20 for some office visits and up to a $50 copayment for emergency room visits that don't result in inpatient admission.

You live in Massachusetts, Minnesota, or Wisconsin

If you live in one of these 3 states, Medigap policies are standardized in a different way.

- You live in Massachusetts
- You live in Minnesota
- You live in Wisconsin

For more information

- Find a Medigap policy.
- Call your State Health Insurance Assistance Program (SHIP).
- Call your State Insurance Department.

The Official U.S. Government Site for Medicare

The Official U.S. Government Site for Medicare

NOW THEN, WHAT EXACTLY IS MEDICAID?

Medicaid is a Federally funded medical insurance plan for low income and disabled individuals. Eligibility is based on the Federal Poverty Level which changes every year. For example, a single elderly person living alone would have an income of $11,880 or below in the year 2016. A couple would have an income of $16,020 or less in 2016 to be considered living below the poverty level.

We could stop there, but alas, you need more information because if the Federal Government could have named Medicaid something completely different like Happycaid, at least we wouldn't continually confuse it with Medicare or Medigap.

Although Medicaid does provide insurance for children, pregnant women, parents, seniors and disabled individuals, for our purposes here, we will only talk about Medicaid for seniors and older disabled individuals.

1. Seniors and Older Disabled Individuals

For the older disabled, Medicaid is a health insurance benefit that may be available to you if you meet certain income and asset restrictions. If you are disabled, and under age 65 (and therefore not yet eligible for Medicare) and your income falls below certain income and asset restrictions you will be given a Medicaid Health Insurance card for your health insurance, because Medicaid is health insurance for poor disabled people.

Once you have been disabled for over 24 months, your health insurance will be converted from Medicaid to Medicare as your new health insurance coverage. If you continue to meet the assets and income tests,(that you have very low income based on the Federal Poverty Levels and you have very little in savings) you can also be on both Medicare as your health insurance and Medicaid as your Medigap coverage and get Extra Help for prescription drug coverage.

If you are 65 years old, you are on Medicare. If you are 65 years old and poor, you are on Medicare and Medicaid. If you are disabled for over 24 months and on Social Security Disability, you are on Medicare regardless of your age. If you also meet the low income and asset test you are on Medicare and Medicaid.

If you are 65 years old and not poor, you are on Medicare for your health insurance and need to have a Medigap policy or be in a Medicare Advantage (Part C) program and also make sure your prescription drugs are covered by either your Medicare Advantage

(Part C) plan, your Medigap policy or you need to add a prescription Medicare Part D (prescription drugs only) plan.

The hot button here is that if you are disabled, have a small income, and very little in savings. Then you get health insurance coverage through Medicaid or, after age 65, a combination of Medicare and Medicaid.

2. How to Hop on Medicaid from Medicare in a Nursing Home Situation

If your loved one enters a nursing home after being hospitalized for 3 days or more (see Chapter Two), and they are currently on Medicare Parts A and B or Medicare Part C (a Medicare Advantage Program) they will have 100 days of coverage paid for by Medicare in the nursing home. But they must enter that nursing home within 30 days of having been in the hospital for the requisite 3 day stay.

If your loved one goes in and out of that nursing home time and time again. The rules get as knotty as a six-way love affair.

If your loved one leaves the nursing home and returns to that or another nursing home within 30 days, your loved one is still on the 100 day clock from the first stay, regardless of why they are back.

If your loved one leaves the nursing home and doesn't return within 30 days and does not have another 3 day stay in the hospital, you are not eligible for Medicare to pay for the nursing home.

If your loved one leaves the nursing home and does not go to the hospital or any nursing home for 60 days, you start a new period of eligibility. This means you need another 3 day stay in the hospital and then you get the 100 days paid for by Medicare.

This can happen as many times as you can calculate 3 days, 30 days and 60 days. As you can imagine, it can get very entangled and cause much wrangling with Medicare. And you can't talk to Medicare about it unless you did all those other things in Chapters One and Two to make sure somebody will talk to you.

And still we are not finished with this can of worms. The paragraph below is directly from the www.medicare.gov website:

> Remember, any days you spend in a hospital as an outpatient (before you're formally admitted as an inpatient based on the doctor's order) aren't counted as inpatient days. An inpatient stay begins on the day you're formally admitted to a hospital with a doctor's order. That's your first inpatient day. The day of discharge doesn't count as an inpatient day.

This paragraph from the Medicare website is critical because hospitals like to play this game where they keep you in the Emergency Room and do not admit you.

They call this *Observation*. You can be in Observation for hours or even sometimes days, and it doesn't count towards your inpatient days. This may be fine, if you think this is a small incident, or this is a temporary problem, and you have no reason to think your loved one needs to be in a nursing home or rehabilitation situation. Observation for some hours or even a day is acceptable. I just had a conversation with a hospital wherein they have instituted a beautiful, calm Observation Unit, outside of the ER, for just this purpose.

However, if you are sure this is a chronic problem and your loved one needs real care for an extended period of time, this is where you, as a caregiver, may need to get ugly. You absolutely must insist that they admit your loved one. If your loved one is seriously ill, and if they cannot determine the cause, or they know the cause, but are just running tests, talk to the doctor in charge. Let her or him know that you want your loved one admitted, not just observed. Let the doctor also know that *you know* if it is necessary for Medicare purposes to get your loved one to rehabilitation or a nursing home, you must get that 3 day clock running. If it appears that your loved one is not going home in a few hours, get cracking on getting them admitted. Because that 3 day stay in a hospital is considered a long-term relationship these days. Almost nobody gets one, everybody wants one, and it's more rare than winning the Mega Bucks lottery.

3. Now Your Loved One is on Medicare and in a Nursing Home

You have successfully gotten your loved one into a fine nursing home for rehabilitation.

You are in the 100 day period, where Medicare is paying for your loved one's care and physical therapy. In some cases, you will get your loved one home and all is well for a while. In other cases, your loved one's health may take a turn for the worse and it looks like your loved one will need to stay in a nursing home for the long haul.

What do you do?

A. You need to assess your loved one's assets. This means you have to look at all their money, accounts, and certain possessions because you will be expected to fill out a form for the nursing home accounting for all these assets.

Now all those times you went to see an Elder Lawyer about issues for yourself or your loved one, you may have done some very good Estate and Elder Law planning. And if you did, that's so good. It means you may be prepared for this moment.

But I understand how that may or may not have happened. You or your loved one may not have been ready to make certain decisions. You may be in a crisis situation that is completely unexpected. Or you may have done all the planning that made sense at the time, but now you have to move forward into the next step that includes nursing home expenses.

In any event, you are here now and you need to know what to do. I will always recommend that you go back to your Elder Lawyer, if you have one, and let them know that the game has changed. You are now looking to go from Medicare to Medicaid in some period of time. That means that you are going to use up those 100 days of Medicare and then have to pay for the nursing home out of your parent's assets. And perhaps, eventually, you will have your parent on Medicaid as they have no more assets to pay for their nursing home care.

So you have to assess your loved one's assets. Then you must decide how to spend those assets in order to do the best for your parent and/or parents in this new situation. Know that Medicaid, the program that pays for long term nursing care, expects you to 'pay down' your assets so that you only have a few thousand dollars in the bank.

How does that happen?

B. You need to get rid of assets.

Now most people would like to believe that they can just give their loved one's money and property away. After all, you wisely became the POA for your loved one. You spoke to an attorney who asked you all the right questions about gifting and you set up the POA so that you could gift as your loved one would want.

Not so fast. The rules surrounding Medicaid eligibility and gifting are pretty strict. And regardless of what you might think, your State and Federal Government are not as stupid as you might want them to be in this situation.

1.) There is the 5 year look back period.

If you or your loved one has gifted away any assets of your loved one in the last 5 years, you are expected to come clean and report that on your application for Medicaid. If that money is needed to take care of your loved one, you are expected to get it back. You need to find it somewhere because you will be penalized for that amount of money and Medicaid will not pay the nursing home bill for the time that amount of money would have covered.

2.) Your loved one may keep his house and one family car and all their basic home goods and furnishings.

3.) Your loved one may also keep one half of the cash assets that are joint with his/her spouse up to $119,220 (this amount changes every year).

4.) All other joint assets with a spouse such as investments, stocks, bonds, savings, checking accounts, vacation homes, are expected to be used to pay for nursing home care.

5.) The spouse who is not in a nursing home is called a Community Spouse.

6.) A Community Spouse can keep her own pension, 401K, IRA'a and Social Security, in some states, but not in all states. Check the laws in your state.

7.) A Community Spouse can only get her spouse's Social Security if she shows a need to have that money to pay her bills. There is Minimum Monthly Needs Allowance. At this writing, that is about $2,000 and there is allegedly a Maximum Monthly Needs Allowance of about $2,900 (and these amounts change every year as well)... all of that is possibly negotiable in some ways. But you need an Elder Lawyer to help you with that. If your loved one or you are the Community Spouse and you need more than the Minimum Monthly Needs Allowance to survive and pay all your bills, you will need to have a hearing before an Administrative Law Judge to be allowed to prove you need it and keep it. There is no way you should attend this hearing without proper preparation from an Elder Lawyer.

As you can see, this is the tip of the iceberg for a scary process. Once someone enters a nursing home and it looks like it will be a permanent solution to a difficult problem, the issues begin to mount.

Any advance planning you have done will be helpful but if you haven't been able to do any advance planning in terms of Medicaid, you can and will do whatever you need to do to make it the best you can.

If you or your loved one is married, we've outlined above what the challenges of staying in a nursing home will be. You need to discuss crisis planning with an Elder Lawyer so you can figure out how to protect and preserve assets for the Community Spouse. If you can have this conversation today before the crisis happens, I strongly encourage you to do so. Now is always a good time to discuss with your Elder Lawyer any strategies for crisis planning. You may not wish to implement all the proposed strategies right away. But you will be informed.

If you or your loved one is single, you are in a different place. The single person in a nursing home is expected to use all of their assets to pay for their care. Careful pre-planning with an Elder lawyer and your financial planner can possibly create certain situations where there might be assets to pass on to family or charity even under these circumstances. Depending on your financial situation it could be possible to leave a legacy to loved ones. But again, pre-planning is best and crisis planning is harder.

None of that means you can't still do planning when the nursing home situation looks permanent. What it does mean is that you may spend much more money on nursing home care, rather than keeping your spouse from poverty or leaving a legacy to your children or family. So all of sudden, that legal bill for estate and elder law planning is worth so much more than it looks.

I know I'm going to hear a lot of criticism for sending people to lawyers. That's okay. The choice is always ultimately yours. The healthcare system and the long term care system have been set up to be a complicated and convoluted process that works harder to take your money than it does to give you great health care. I will always err on the side of good planning and good advice. The best advice I can ever give you is to get good advice…because that's good planning that will save you money in the long run.

CHAPTER THREE

MONEY OFTEN COSTS TOO MUCH....Ralph Waldo Emerson

Pity the Pittas

In 2011, the Supreme Court of Pennsylvania declined to help John Pittas. John was a good son, who believed his step-father and even perhaps his two siblings should help out with Mom's big, huge $93,000 nursing home bill.

The nursing home sued John because, hey, why not? We have his name here in the file as her son. John comes here to visit his mom and seems to have a car and nice clothes. John can probably afford to pay a $93,000 bill all by himself, that he didn't incur. There must be an old law somewhere that can help us get that money out of John.

John did what every self-respecting son does. He applied for Medicaid to pay for his mom's nursing home bill. But nobody wanted to wait for that. The nursing home just sued John. John's mom, Mrs. Pittas, went to Greece with her husband and left John in Pennsylvania. The nursing home could have sued John's stepdad, but he was in Greece too. So that was way too complicated and troublesome. Besides, John earned $85,000 a year. The court decided that was more than enough to take on this $93,000 balance from Mom's nursing home care.

In March of 2013, The Supreme Court of Pennsylvania was really, really busy. They just had to let some things go. One of them was <u>Health Care & Ret. Corp. of Am. v. Pittas</u>, 2012 PA Super 96, 46 A.3d 719, 723 (Pa. Super. Ct. 2012), reargument denied (July 18, 2012),<u>appeal denied,</u> 63 A.3d 1248 (Pa. 2013).

So as it stands now, pity the Pittas who tried to take care of his mom, and got taken to the cleaners instead.

MONEY

This topic is the one nobody wants to talk about. Yet, everyone should have talked about it over and over and over again.

The average cost of a nursing home in Pennsylvania is $10,000 per month. If you enter a nursing home, and you are now paying for it, you are fully expected to pay that $10,000 per month out of your assets.

1. Caregivers and Money

As a caregiver of your parents, your brother, your grandmom or even your spouse, you need to have the hard conversation about money. This is how money works when you are disabled and living in my state, of Pennsylania. It can be a bit better or even much worse in other states. Each state is different and can make their own rules.

A. Disabled Spouses and Money

If your husband or wife is disabled and you are their caregiver, in the world of Medicare and Medicaid, the fact that you are spouses *does not give you access to all your spouse's assets as if they are your own.*

So, for example, if you use your husband's Social Security check to pay for housing expenses, heat, electricity, water and sewer, perhaps even a mortgage, groceries, gas and cable TV, and you use your Social Security check for chocolate, golf outings, new shoes, trips to the Casino and Friday night pizza, you've got a new sheriff in town.

If your husband is now the disabled person, and he enters a nursing home, it is fully expected that any and all assets that are in his name only, or are his income only will be used to defray the cost of the nursing home.

There are some exceptions:

1.) You can keep your house

When one spouse is in a facility and the other is at home, the spouse at home is referred to as the Community Spouse. If you are at home, you should change the deed on your house so that the Community Spouse immediately becomes the sole owner. This is legitimate, it is not considered abuse of the system, and any nursing home worth its salt, as my Nana used to say, will tell you this. The minute your disabled spouse enters a nursing home on a permanent basis, the deed to your home should be signed over to the Community Spouse. Since you have your Power of Attorney documents in order, you should be able to do this with no problem.

2.) You can keep one car

The Feds and everyone else figures you need to drive, at least to the nursing home and back, so yeah, you can have some wheels. However, if you each have a car, and your spouse is not coming home and you need to pay for his care, you will have to sell the second car. And not for a dollar to your nephew, you will need to sell it for a legitimate price.

3.) You can keep your stuff

And by 'stuff' they mean clothing, jewelry, furniture, pets, computers, books, furs, Waterford crystal, diamond watches, pots and pans. The nursing home police are not coming into your house to see what kinds of possessions you have. They are most interested in the topic of this chapter....*money*.

4.) Other stuff

There are other exceptions, like things you use for your business. Most people are affected by the top three here. And this is where a good Elder Lawyer comes in. Find her or him and talk to them. Know what you can and cannot do and when you can and cannot do it. Knowledge is Power.

Now…what you can't keep, what you can't give away, and what you have to get back.

Once your spouse enters a nursing home on a permanent basis, you will be expected to pay for their care from your assets either right away or after the 100 days that Medicare will pay for the nursing home under certain circumstances (See Chapter Two).

You will be given an Admissions Notice Packet and asked to file a form that's called a Resource Assessment Form. The whole purpose of these forms is to have you record every possible place where you may have funds available to divide between the person in the nursing home and the Community Spouse for living expenses.

Generally, they will look at the 'pot' and divide it in half to start. That's just the starting point. The 'pot' is not your monthly income from pensions, annuities, or Social Security. The 'pot' is all your other assets that are cash or can be turned into cash. Like, cash, stocks, bonds, 410Ks, annuities that aren't paying out a monthly amount, Christmas clubs, trusts, trust funds, mutual funds, savings bonds from your wedding 30 years ago, stuff like that.

Once they divide the pot in half, they look at the Community Spouse's expenses and decide how much she can keep. There is a maximum amount that is, at this writing, $119,220. If you can show that your household and living expenses require you to keep more than that, and you actually have more than that, you may be able to keep it. However, *how you keep it gets a little tricky.*

And this is where a good Elder Lawyer comes in. Find her or him and talk to them. Know what you can and cannot do and when you can and cannot do it. Knowledge is Power.

We haven't even discussed monthly income, because that is not a part of the 'pot.'

At first glance, your spouse's monthly income goes to the nursing home and you get to keep yours. Big Whoop! There are very few spouses who are living solely on their own income. Moreover, this is where, you as a woman, if you are the Community Spouse, gets punished for all those years of child-rearing, being a caregiver to your Mom and Dad, fighting to break the glass ceiling, having an in-and-out career that left your Social Security in tatters, gave you little or no pension, and made you dependent upon your husband's income for the golden years to be the good life for both of you. Yeah, that's over. And it's painful.

I have counseled many a client in these shoes. The husbands who have come my way, where their wife is the one in the nursing home and they are the Community Spouse, very rarely suffer the financial depths and despair of their female counterparts. That 21 cents less that every woman is still making is much more than 21 cents, it can lead to an elder life of poverty. Because this is the expectation from the Feds and the State.

You need to prove that you need more than about $2,000 a month. This is known as the Minimum Monthly Needs Allowance. They will let you keep that much from a combination of yours and your nursing home spouse's monthly income. Everything over and above that you don't get to keep unless you can prove you need it.

It can go something like this.

Jane and Jerry Doe are married 52 years. Jane is 73 years old and John is 75 years old. Jerry suffers a debilitating stroke just after they return from their Viking Cruise in Russia. Up until this point, Jane and Jerry were enjoying their retirement with travel, grandchildren, dinners and golf at the club, theater tickets and even an active sex life! So this set back is a shock to their system. They have never consulted an Elder Lawyer, but at the prodding of their kids, they do have Wills, Powers of Attorney, and Living Wills. They do not have Long Term Care Insurance and they let their life insurance lapse because they no longer had young children to worry about.

The first days in the hospital are filled with high emotions, many questions and much dread. In the next week or so, it appears that the stroke is extremely debilitating and Jerry will have to go to a rehabilitation facility in the very least to see how many activities of daily living he can recover. At this point, Jerry needs to be dressed, bathed, fed, and pushed around in a wheelchair. It's not good.

It doesn't get better. Jerry has a few more mini-strokes in the nursing home and it looks like this will become his permanent home. Jane and all her family are devastated.

Jane goes with her son to an Elder Lawyer.

Jane takes home $1,113 per month in Social Security. This is basically Jane's 'play money.' Jerry's Social Security is $2,226 per month, which they use for their household expenses. Jerry gets a pension of $2,000 a month. He also has a 401K worth $550,000. They have a mutual fund account of $230,000. And the rest of their assets are two cars, their house, and a few savings bonds they collected over the years, worth about $5,000.

Jane can show that even though she no longer has a mortgage, her household expenses for heat, water, sewer, taxes and upkeep, as well as groceries, prescriptions, and ongoing medical expenses create a legitimate need for her to have $2,400 per month. The nursing home will allow her to keep $1387 of Jerry's Social Security check towards her expenses. She is expected to turn over the rest of the Social Security and all of the pension check money to the nursing home for Jerry's care.

Additionally, Jane can keep half of the rest of the assets but not to exceed $119,220. The rest is expected to be used for Jerry's care.

On the face of it, Jane is expected to live the next 20 years or so on the $2,400 she qualifies for, and her savings are now a paltry

> And this is where a good Elder Lawyer comes in. Find her or him and talk to them. Know what you can and cannot do and when you can and cannot do it. Knowledge is Power.

$119,220.....for the rest of her life. There are options here to help Jane which are legal and complicated.

The other thing I want you to know here is this. If the tables were turned and Jane was the spouse in the nursing home, Jerry gets to keep all of his Social Security, all of his monthly pension, all of his 401K, no questions asked. That money is considered Jerry's and not Jane's and is not payable to the nursing home. This is true in some states, but not all. All Jerry would lose is Jane's monthly Social Security and about half of the mutual fund. That's the price you pay for being a stay-at-home Mom, a caregiver, a housewife, and even if you worked all your life, but were underpaid.

The other thing that could help Jane here is if Jane and Jerry had purchased Long Term Care Insurance (See Chapter One). Long Term Care Insurance could be used to defray the cost of a nursing home. This gives Jane time to move assets around, legally, so that she will have more money in her future.

After you have recorded every possible financial asset, this paragraph below changes the game in ways most of you have not yet discovered.

> Within the past 60 months, have you or your spouse closed, given away, sold or transferred any assets such as: a home, land, personal property, life insurance

policies, annuities bank accounts, certificates of deposit, stocks, IRA, bonds or a right to income? Within the past 60 months, have you or your spouse transferred any assets into a trust?

Because after all the time in the hospital with your ill spouse, all the time trying to find a rehabilitation center and nursing home that you feel comfortable with, all the time you've spent crying, praying and on the phone with doctors, insurance companies and your kids, now they want to know what have you given away or sold in the last five years that can be reclaimed to pay for your spouses' care. Yeah, it's that kind of crap.

Why do they want to know this and when? Why they want to know this is because you can't just be giving away your money to your kids now that you have a $10,000 a month nursing home bill and you don't want to pay it. The nursing home wants to know right away, but here's the kicker. If you can pay for five years of nursing home care using that Long Term Care Insurance and the monthly income and assets you have, anything over and above that you may be able to give away or at least use to make some investments for you, the Community Spouse to make your life bearable and liveable no matter what comes. This is complicated. Not nearly as simple as these black words and white spaces.

And this is where a good Elder Lawyer comes in. Find her or him and talk to them. Know what you can and cannot do and when you can and cannot do it. Knowledge is Power.

B. Parents and Money

So what is different when it's Parents and Money and not Spouses and Money. Well, if your parents have money, and they are spouses listen to the section above. If you only have one parent living, it's a bit of a different story.

In the case where Mom is still living, but Dad has passed away, you as the caregiver have the responsibilities as the Power of Attorney. You have to make the financial and health decisions either alone or with a sibling, aunt, uncle or cousin, whoever your parent appointed as Power of Attorney.

The first thing you should do is carefully read the Power of Attorney which will give you come clues as to how to deal with your parent's money. The POA will likely allow you to make all forms of financial transactions such as simple banking, stock transfers or sales, cashing of mutual funds, annuities or any other kind of investment accounts. Good. You need to be able to do those things for your mom. You need to be able to pay her nursing home bills, get her wheelchair fixed, take her to the hairdresser, buy her new shoes, and pay for a home health aide if you take her to a doctor's appointment.

Keep reading that POA. Now look at any and all provisions that have to do with gifting. First, know that if mom is elderly, in a nursing home, or looking at some kind of assisted living in the future, or just has health issues, you need to know that your gifting days are over. Remember that 5 year look back period we talked about earlier? If Mom is 92 or even 72 but in seriously ill health, and you end up placing her in a nursing home where you think you're going to get Uncle Sam to pay for it, think again. It is far too late to go into panic mode and try and quickly give away $14,000 to each and every sibling, their spouses and their children before you have to pay a nursing home bill. The only way that will work is if you have money in excess of the cost of 5 years of nursing home bills (which would be around $600,000 on average).

But, even if Mom has 600K, you may not have permission to gift away a dime of it. The gifting provisions in POAs have come under great scrutiny in the last years because of financial abuse of elders. Too many POAs, whether they were children, caregivers, neighbors, or the pizza guy, have been found to take advantage of elderly people and steal their money, leaving the senior citizen penniless and with no assets for their care. Consequently, legislatures all over the country have made sure provisions in POAs concerning gifting are explicit in what you can and cannot do.

If you have no power to gift in that POA, don't even try it. Remember, the nursing home needs to see all these documents both financial and legal. They will do all in their power to get their payment first, before you, before your daughter's college, before Disneyworld. If you gifted and you couldn't, you are going to be expected to give that money back to pay for Mom's care. Be careful.

> And this is where a good Elder Lawyer comes in. Find her or him and talk to them. Know what you can and cannot do and when you can and cannot do it. Knowledge is Power.

The big difference with a single person, whether it be you or your parent is that there is no Community Spouse to worry about. But the other side of that coin is that since there is no Community Spouse to worry about, all money is fully expected to be paid to the nursing home for Mom's care.

If Mom has a house, you don't have to sell it immediately. You just tell the nursing home you think Mom will return home. It doesn't matter if that's a practical impossibility, you can just say that's what you want, and it effectively cuts off the sale of Mom's house until she passes away. And that's when the Executor (remember "once you pass away only an Executor can play") will be expected to sell Mom's house and reimburse the government for any money paid to the nursing home for Mom's care.

There are other exceptions to selling Mom's house. Some include: if an adult child has lived there for over a year and is on the deed, if there are children under 18 in the house, if there is a disabled child living there. These exceptions change the rules about whether the money from the sale of the house needs to go to the nursing home after Mom's death. But it's not easy, as are rules about Estate Recovery, which we will discuss below.

And this is where a good Elder Lawyer comes in. Find her or him and talk to them. Know what you can and cannot do and when you can and cannot do it. Knowledge is Power.

Any other money Mom has outside of her house such as her bank accounts, her monthly income from Social Security, Dad's pension, her 401K, her annuities, her whole-life life insurance policy, all of that is expected to be used for her care until you "spend down" her assets to either $8,000 or $2,400 depending on her monthly income (it could be more or less depending on which state you live in,)

Don't try and keep it for yourself. Don't have a big family meeting to decide how to divide up Mom's accounts so that Medicare (someone will say Medicare, but it's Medicaid who pays the nursing home bill. See Chapter Two), will pay her bill. Don't give her car to the grandson going to college, unless he's going to pay full Blue Book price for it. Don't do any of it. If you've waited until she's in a nursing home. Get some good advice, but don't do anything because you think you can beat the system because you can't. You can't beat it and you will pay for trying.

This is where you will need to be or become a good record keeper. You will need to account for the funds Mom spends. You will be expected to show months of bank statements and financial records to a nursing home so that they can determine if your parent qualifies for Medicaid.

You also need to keep abreast of Mom's finances so that you are aware of when she may be running out of funds to pay for her care. That is the critical time to apply for Medicaid. This is discussed in Chapter Two and just a reminder here. Once you are in charge of Mom's money, especially if you see needing care in her future, you must be accountable and informed about what you can do with her funds.

FILIAL SUPPORT LAW

The tale at the beginning of this chapter was meant to grab your attention about all the crazy things that can happen in this Elder Law arena. It was a cautionary tale about something called Filial Support or Filial Responsibility Laws. As of this writing, 30 states have a law which says in one way or another, the state can sue you for the bills of your indigent elderly parents. These laws, almost in their entirety, date back to the 19th century or even earlier, and yet they are still on the books, or have been revived. A few states, mine included, Pennsylvania, have invoked these laws to collect money back from children where the state spent funds on their parent for nursing home care.

So it's out there, folks. It's a dirty trick, but you need to know about it.

I advise everyone who asks, when you sign papers as a POA for your parent as they enter a nursing home or assisted living facility, *always, always, always put the letters "POA" behind your signature...like this*

Cathleen S. Sikorski, POA for Mom Sikorski

And sign on the Signature Line for the person entering the nursing home. Remember, as POA, you are *legally acting as if you are the person you represent.* If the nursing home documents have a signature line like this:

_____never sign here.

(Responsible Party)

YOU ARE NOT THE RESPONSIBLE PARTY AS THE POA.

There was a time when a person who signed as the "Responsible Party" could be held contractually liable for the nursing home resident's bill. And then there was a time when that was outlawed. Now we seem to have entered a time warp. Administratively, the federal government has tinkered with these rules and that, in combination with the Filial Support Laws, has brought down all kinds of cockamamie results. The current 30 states with Filial Support Laws are:

Alaska, Arkansas, California, Connecticut, Delaware, Georgia, Idaho, Indiana, Iowa, Kentucky, Louisiana, Maryland, Massachusetts, Mississippi, Montana, Nevada, New Hampshire, New Jersey, North Carolina, North Dakota, Ohio, Oregon, Pennsylvania, Rhode Island, South Dakota, Tennessee, Utah, Vermont, Virginia, and West Virginia.

The cockamamie results are that some states can and have sued adult children for their parent's nursing home bills. Some states have the legal right to take criminal action against adult children who won't pay. And most states are leaving it alone not trying to put the fun into dysfunction by pitting siblings against each other, while taking care of Mom's five billion other issues as she is puttering around in a nursing home.

What can you do about this? You could move to one of the other 20 states, other than that, just don't sign as the "Responsible Party", spend your parent's assets appropriately, don't give away the candy store to anyone, and keep your nose clean. Basically, take your Mother's advice as she sent you off to kindergarten. None of that is a guarantee, because Mr. Pittas tried all those things and so far it has not worked out for him.

C. SINGLE PEOPLE AND MONEY

Single people and money have much in common with your single parent and money. The most significant difference is if you're a single person and not elderly. I have been the caregiver for a friend who had a Traumatic Brain Injury when she fell down a flight of stairs at age 57. She was a vital, active, working woman at the time of her accident. She had a small stint in a rehabilitation center and has lived very successfully on her own since then. But she desperately needed a POA both in her emergency status and even now. She is collecting Social Security Disability and has qualified for Medicare as a disabled person under the age of 65. She is eligible for certain services and financial benefits that are not usually attributed to younger people. If she ever does enter a nursing home, we will be sure and implement the strategies here for a single person.

I was also the primary caregiver for my brother-in-law for seven years as he suffered from Multiple Sclerosis. He, too was under 65 when that journey began. He entered nursing homes for rehabilitation more times than I can count. Every single time I signed those documents, I placed the letters POA after my name. I never once signed as "Responsible Party." Some nursing homes had "Responsible Party" on the signature line and others did not. But I always signed on the line where my brother-in-law would have signed and merely put my POA designation.

As to his funds, I did everything I could to save a significant amount for his care, because his children were in no way financially capable of paying for his care, and none of them resided in the state where he lived, my brother-in-law and I made a plan to use his funds for his care and keep him in a home-like setting as long as possible.

My brother-in-law very much wanted to leave some kind of funds to his children and he was able to do that quite nicely. We talked about it many times, discussed it with his financial advisor and made adjustments along the way, as his care became more complicated and expensive.

As you can see from this, every single case is different. Which is why......

> And this is where a good Elder Lawyer comes in. Find her or him and talk to them. Know what you can and cannot do and when you can and cannot do it. Knowledge is Power.

D. DISABLED CHILDREN AND MONEY

Although I would very much like to include a section here on Disabled Children and Money, this is not my forte. I have no real contact with this area of expertise. What I do know is that it requires great planning and often leads to the creation of Special Needs Trusts. These Special Needs Trusts are also a tool often used with adults who become disabled at a relatively young age from those horrific diseases like Alzheimer's, ALS, MS or who are the victims of accidents.

There are really fine lawyers who make this part of their legal practice a priority and do a great job in preserving assets for young and/or permanently disabled people. Call your local Bar Association and ask for a referral. Ask friends who have dealt with a disabled person. Within support groups for these particular diseases you can bet there are people who have found a lawyer who works in this field. Those support groups can often be found through your local hospital. Find those groups and use them, they are a great resource.

> And this is where a good Elder Lawyer comes in. Find her or him and talk to them. Know what you can and cannot do and when you can and cannot do it. Knowledge is Power.

E. ESTATE RECOVERY

Estate Recovery is what happens when your loved one passes away. If your caregivee has entered a nursing home during the time you've been caring for him or her, and if you had to file for Medicaid benefits to pay for their care while they were in that nursing home, your loved one's estate is subject to Estate Recovery.

What is Estate Recovery?

The state in which you live is entitled to ask for all of the Medicaid money spent on your loved one's behalf in a nursing home to be returned to the state. If there is any money in your loved one's estate, one of the first in line to be repaid is the bill your loved one has accrued in that nursing home.

Where does that bill come from?

The minute you ask for Medicaid benefits, that bill begins to generate. Here's how it happens. You spend weeks, months, maybe even years working on the plan to spend down Mom's assets so that she can qualify for Medicaid. Remember, Medicaid is that plan that pays for the nursing home when you run out of money.

Once your Mom is on Medicaid, you are probably sending them the funds that you receive from her Social Security check (or it is automatically going to the nursing home right from Social Security). You are sending them any additional monthly funds you may be receiving from a pension, annuity or other income. You are keeping her savings to the permitted $2400 or $8000 maximum allowed and no more.

But you haven't sold Mom's house and Mom passes away.

The only assets you have in Mom's estate are her house and the $8,000 that she was permitted to keep in a savings account..

The State spent $100,000 keeping your Mom in that nursing home for 18 months.

Guess what?

The State wants it $100,000 back, or at least as much of it as it can get. Where will that $100,000 come from? It will come from the sale of Mom's house and any excess money from her savings account.

Are there other people who can get paid first, before you have to return that $100,000? Yes, there are quite a few people who come first, but you're not one of them. So don't think you will be giving that money to you and your brother and sister as your inheritance. That is not what is going to happen.

Here's a list of the things that get paid for first in Pennsylvania:

Funeral expenses

Administration expenses (including court fees, accountants, legal fees, etc.)

Taxes (federal and state)

Expenses of last illness

Here's where you pay the nursing home back, either as an expense of last illness or in a category of its own. Expense of last illness would include any payments due to hospitals, doctors, co-pays for prescription drugs, any other medical providers for such things as durable medical equipment. Technically the nursing home would come after those bills are paid.

All other debts

And even those "all other debts" have an order of priority. All of this assumes you have enough money to pay every single bill. You might have the money and you might not.

Then comes the art of negotiation.

When my brother-in-law passed away, I had a dispute with several of his medical providers. Those disputes actually began before he died, but continued after his death. I had the money to pay those bills, but my allegiance was to the Estate and ultimately the beneficiaries. I negotiated those payments down to what I thought was fair and reasonable and what I would have paid if my brother-in-law were still living and arguing about what he owed.

Just because someone dies, does not mean he has to pay bills without questioning their authenticity.

Once you've paid all the required expenses, if you can reimburse the state for the money they paid out on your Mom's behalf you must do so. In fact, in Pennsylvania, you are required by law, if your loved one has been in a nursing home to write a letter to the Department of Human Services asking…"Hey, does my Mom owe you any money?" They are required to answer you within 30 days (hey thanks for asking…no you don't or yeah, you do and here's how much).

And this amount is negotiable as well if there are limited funds in your mom's estate. But if there are sufficient funds to pay all the expenses of the Estate and pay back the nursing home bill, you will be expected to do so. The good news is, if there's any left over, you get to divide the remaining funds according to your mom's will. (Of course, your mom has a will…see Chapter One…because unlike Prince your mom got her act together and got her affairs in order like the smart lady she is!).

F. FUNERAL EXPENSES

1. Prepaid Funeral Arrangements

One great planning tool that everyone should take advantage of is pre-planning a funeral. Check to see if your state has guarantees as to any money you would pay in advance for a funeral. States have different requirements and protections. Although, the Federal Trade Commission has some rules and regulations https://www.consumer.ftc.gov/articles/0070-shopping-funeral-services you must do your homework. By Federal law all funeral homes must give you prices over the phone so you can comparison shop. That's a start.

Elder Lawyers recommend pre-paying for a funeral so that if your loved one dies with no real assets, you don't then have to worry that you can't pay for a funeral as well. It also is an allowable expense in order to qualify for Medicaid. There is no penalty for paying money for a funeral in order to get Medicaid to start paying a nursing home bill. You would hate to be consumed with grief, estate matters, excess medical bills, and have no money for a funeral. But you must do your homework. Ask good questions, some of which follow here, put out by the FTC to protect consumers who are seeking to prepay for a funeral.

- What happens to the money you've prepaid?
    States have different requirements for handling funds paid for prearranged funeral services.
- What happens to the interest income on money that is prepaid and put into a trust account?
- Are you protected if the firm you dealt with goes out of business?
- Can you cancel the contract and get a full refund if you change your mind?
- What happens if you move to a different area or die while away from home?
    Some prepaid funeral plans can be transferred but often at an added cost.

2. Irrevocable Burial Bank Account

You can open an irrevocable burial account in your bank or credit union in Pennsylvania (and some other states). If you make that call to the funeral homes and have them quote a price to you or send you a list of prices, you can decide how much money to put aside for a funeral in your irrevocable burial trust account. Just go to your bank or credit union and tell them that's the type of account you want to open. They do it all the time. It's not a new idea. It's just that no one knows that banks and credit unions have such an account. And no one knows they need to open an irrevocable burial account when a nursing home is on the horizon for them or their loved one.

There's so much more one could say about money, and yet, there's never enough...to say, and money. Sigh...we are all just doing our best. Which is why we need to take care of ourselves.

CHAPTER FOUR

ARE YOU SOCIALLY SECURE?

You've probably all seen a Social Security Card. It's on a lovely blue background and has your name and Social Security Number on it. It is likely that you've seen a Medicare Card as well. It may have been your mother's or your father's card, if you are not yet in the prime of your life to be receiving Medicare benefits.

You may have noticed that a Medicare card is red, white and blue, like the American flag. So nice. You may have also noticed that a person's Medicare Number and Social Security Number are exactly the same. Sometimes Medicare Numbers have a suffix letter, but the number is the identical number as the recipient's Social Security Number. This is basically true for everyone on the planet.

The following is a conversation I had with the Medicare Appeal Board:

"Do you have the Social Security Number of the person who is appealing?"

"Sorry, I don't."

"That's okay. Do you have their Medicare Number instead?"

I rest my case.

SOCIAL SECURITY

It used to be so easy. You turned 65, you went to the Social Security Office when there was one on every Main Street, you signed up and boom! You were on Medicare and you started getting your Social Security check every month.

Not so much anymore.

Like the cashier in the grocery store, no one knows how to deal with all the change in Social Security.

We will try to give you enough information to dilute some of the complexities. But here's the key: Every person reading this has a different financial situation. You may have two or three different financial situations, one for you and your spouse and one for your loved one, as their caregiver. Social Security is a *financial decision* that will literally affect you the rest of your life. It requires some time, research and thought. There are many financial experts who have good information on Social Security. If you have a financial planner, you should discuss this with that person. But make sure, and ask your financial planner, if they know the rules about Medicaid...not Medicare....Medicaid.

If you have an Elder Lawyer, whom you previously consulted, go back and talk to them about Social Security. But ask them if they know about all the ins and outs of Social Security. If not ask them who the expert is who they consult. Then have your financial person speak to your Elder Lawyer.

I am a big fan of personal research, as long as you understand it and ultimately contact an expert for verification.

I cannot put all the permutations of Social Security choices in one short chapter. Many have written 500 page books on this topic alone. And the rules keep changing. So we will look at a few things here. We will remember that things keep changing, and we will research, consult and decide based on each of our own personal financial situations. Capisce? (that's my Italian Grandma Lucy talkin' to you).

Social Security is not an entitlement. You paid for it. So making this singular decision is very important. One year from whenever you make this decision, it becomes irreversible. It is likely the only guaranteed income you will have for the rest of your life.

The first thing you should do is go to www.ssa.gov and set up your own "my account." This is so that you have access to all the information in your Social Security Account from the very first day you began working. My personal account goes all the way back to when I was 16 years old.

The experts will tell you to make certain that the amounts you earned are correct. If you can prove they are incorrect or some years where you earned money are missing, because there is a big fat zero there, get it fixed. Because the way they calculate your Social Security paycheck is to take your 35 top earning years and divide by 420 (the number of months in 35 years). So your highest earning years are your best friends. And if you want to continue to add to that just keep working as long as you can.

The other factor is we *are* living longer. You will need as much as you can get for as long as you can get it. Yes, it's a crapshoot. But if you have the assets or the health or both to build up that Social Security account to a nice healthy flow, once you reach Full Retirement Age, you won't regret it. There is a greater risk in living too long than there is in dying too young when it comes to Social Security.

I know the other thing that scares you is that Social Security is broke and you will wait to sign up and the well will be dry. This concern has some validity. As of this writing, the projections are that the Fund will run pretty dry by 2034, which is almost 20 years from now. For those of us retiring now and even in the next 10 years or so, I say lead with the information you have now. There's no telling where it will go, but the chances of being 'grandfathered in' at a much higher rate or even taking a 'pay cut' on your Social Security is a better prospect. Taking a pay cut on a big check is better than taking a pay cut on a small check. Just sayin'.

Many people think that they should take Social Security as soon as they reach age 62. And perhaps you should, but to do so, you take about a 30% pay cut forever. If you can't afford to wait any longer then take it. That's fine. If you can afford to wait, you should probably do so. At Full Retirement Age there is no pay cut. If you wait a few more years *after* Full Retirement Age and begin to take your Social Security at age 70 there is a 132% raise…..forever. So there's that. But there is no point in waiting after age 70. All bets are off. Age 70 is the magic number and whatever your benefit is at that time is written in stone. Unless you keep working.

If you take your Social Security at age 62 (or any time before your Full Retirement Age) and keep working. You will be penalized. First, you might have to pay income tax on some of that Social Security. If you are an individual and earn $25,000 or more, or you are married and file jointly and earn $32,000 or more in adjusted gross income you might have to pay income tax on some of that Social Security.

If you take your Social Security at age 62 (or any time before your Full Retirement Age) and keep working your benefit check will be reduced $1 for every $2 you earn above $15,720. So if you are taking early to add to your income, you may not really be doing that. And you permanently put your Social Security check at a much lower rate.

This is why you need to consult with an expert. Already you can see how this will affect you and your family for the rest of your life.

SO WHAT EXACTLY IS MY FULL RETIREMENT AGE AND WHAT DO I DO WITH THAT?

That seems like an easy question. But this is Social Security. Get out your calculator. No, just kidding, but here's the deal:

1. If you were born between 1943 and 1954, your full retirement age is 66 years old.

2. If you were born between 1955 and 1959, your full retirement age is between 66 and 67 years old. So for example, if you were born in 1957, your full retirement age is 66 and 6 months.

3. If you were born in 1960 or thereafter, your full retirement age is 67 years old.

I encourage you to look around the website www.ssa.gov for many reasons. There is also a full retirement age calculator there.

Okay, so now you know your Full Retirement Age (FRA). The world of elder care is full of acronyms.

Once you know your FRA, you can decide how to proceed.

- Do you want to look at taking Social Security Benefits at age 62?

- Are you still working at age 62 and so taking Social Security benefits would not help, especially because of the income tax?

- Do you have other assets that will work to pay your bills until Full Retirement Age?

- Would you be able to wait until age 70 to start taking Social Security benefits and then take that sweet 8% per year addition to your Social Security check?

And then it gets tricky.

Now you need to look at Spousal Benefits.

There used to be something called File and Suspend. And it was a nice way to get spousal benefits into your home and add to your income. But that was terminated as of April 30, 2016. So we are leaving it behind.

If you turned 62 no later than January 2, 2016, you have until January of 2020, at least as of this writing, for a restricted spousal benefit.

First, your spouse cannot collect benefits on your record unless you file for your own Social Security. Once you file for your own Social Security, your spouse can collect the spousal share, which is one-half of your amount. This doesn't take any money away from you. It's just a calculation.

This tactic is probably best used when one spouse has higher earnings than the other. The higher earning spouse should wait until he/she turns 70 to collect the highest possible Social Security check. But in the meantime, the lower earning spouse could file for retirement benefits. Once the lower earning spouse has filed, the higher earning spouse can then file a restricted application and the higher earning spouse can take only his/her spousal share. Then at 70 years old, the higher earning spouse goes off of restriction and starts taking his/her full retirement. At which time the lower earning spouse can *now* file for his/her spousal share of the higher earning spouse (likely increasing their social security check!).

Whew!!! Got that??? But that restricted benefit is only for a few with that above birthdate. For the rest of us, you need to look at yours and your spouse's income and assets to figure out the game wisely. There's lots of experts out there who really do want to help you. Find them. You can see why spending some money to get advice makes this work best for you and is so worth it.

If you don't fall in those dates above for using the restricted application. Then you just need to do the calculations. Bottom line is Social Security is a big math problem. Below are a few calculators you can use to make some initial calculations, one of which is on the Social Security website. See....good stuff there!

Retirement Benefits Calculators.

http://maximizemysocialsecurity.com

http://www.aarp.org/work/social-security/social-security-benefits-calculator/

http://www.ssa.gov/planners/benefitcalculators.html

DIVORCED AND SURVIVOR'S BENEFITS

Spousal Benefits for Divorced Spouses

This is an often missed benefit by those who reach full retirement age.

This benefit is available to all ex-spouses. You must be at least 62 years of age, still unmarried and divorced for at least two years. Finally, you had to have been married for at least 10 years prior to your divorce.

Both ex-spouses can collect benefits on each other's work record once you reach full retirement age. AND.....you can still postpone taking your own retirement benefit until you reach age 70, if that makes the most economic sense in your situation.

However, if you apply for spousal benefits before your own full retirement age, you will be forced to apply for retirement benefits under your own work record, that's could be a lesser amount of monthly income. That's why these calculators are so important.

If you have more than one ex-spouse, you can choose the work record of the ex-spouse that gives you the highest benefit. Again, as long as you were married to all those ex-spouses for at least 10 years.

You have to examine this choice carefully. Make sure you are choosing what works for your situation. And know the rules.

And just to make you feel better, especially if your ex-spouse is not your favorite person, he/she will never know that you applied for ex-spouse benefits. No one tells them. It does not affect your ex-spouse's benefit in any way.

SPOUSAL BENEFITS FOR SURVIVING SPOUSES

Again, this is an often missed benefit. I once worked in a non-law setting with a great lady, who had been a widow for many years. When she indicated that times were financially challenging, I asked her if she was receiving widow's benefits from Social Security.

Even working full time, and taking a deduction in her benefit as she earned a bit too much by the end of the year, she still received a benefit that made a significant change in her lifestyle. She could breathe a financial sigh of relief.

This benefit depends on when the survivor claims the benefit. Claiming early reduces you and your survivor's benefit.

You can claim survivor's benefits as early as age 60. And if your financial health depends on that claim, then go ahead and do it. And if you have minor children, you are eligible for a benefit for them as well.

However, if you can wait to claim the survivors benefit until your full retirement age, you will receive the full deceased spouse's benefit.

The point here is that, there are benefits that go unclaimed all the time. I heard a tale recently where a couple went into the Social Security Office and the wife had not worked since they had been married more than 40 years ago. She had no idea she was eligible for spousal benefits. She had left several years of benefits on the table because she did not know there was such a thing as spousal benefits.

This is true for widows, divorced spouses and older individuals with minor children. It is a system with many untapped benefits. The Social Security website is a good starting place. It may be a godsend to many to find out that they are eligible for a monthly benefit for the rest of their lives that they never knew existed.

Remember that story that began this chapter? You might even be smarter than the person who answers the phone!

PART II--CAREGIVING

CHAPTER FIVE

NOW WILL YOU TALK TO ME?

A Discussion with John Hancock

One day a letter came from John Hancock (not the real one, I'm pretty sure he died a while ago) stating that my brother-in-law had a small long term care insurance policy in effect left over from his employment.

Every little bit helps.

So I called John Hancock to see how we could begin using the benefits, as he clearly qualifies based on the policy I had them send to me for review.

"Hello? I would like to file a claim for long term care benefits."

"Ok, I need to ask a few questions," said the nice polite young lady from John Hancock.

"Who are you?" she asked.

"I am his sister-in-law and his Power of Attorney."

"Well, ok, you need to send us a copy of the POA."

"Yes, I can do that, in the meantime can you send me the application for benefits."

"Yes, I will send it to his address."

At that point, I noticed that they had the wrong zip code for his address.

"I see you have the correct street address, but the wrong zip code. Can you correct that before you send it?"

"Oh, no, I'm sorry, I can't change anything of his until you send me the POA."

"But if you send it out, it will go to the wrong place."

"Oh, yes, I see that. Well, would you like me to send the documents to your address?"

I pause for just a nano second, because experience has told me not to interrupt the ridiculous if it is in my favor.

"Yeah, sure, send it directly to me."

I gave her my address.

"Now will you be filing that within one week?" she asked me.

"Well, he's in the hospital for a few days, and may go to a nursing home for rehab or he may come directly home and rehab there, " I told her.

"Oh, well then you have to call back and request the forms after he gets home."

"But it's long term care insurance," I said, "either way he will be under long term care."

"I'm sorry, but I can't send the forms until he's home."

"So," I say through tears.....of laughter, "you can't send the forms for long term care until he's home and not in long term care. And then you can send it to my address until I get you a copy of the POA to correct his address."

"Yes!" she says brightly, that's exactly correct!"

For seven years, I was the primary caregiver for my brother-in-law. He suffered terribly from progressive Multiple Sclerosis. Five years before he died, he was confined to an electric wheelchair and bed. Larry was a curmudgeon by birth, but in a very funny and entertaining way. He never, and I mean never, gave me the 'why me' story. He joked often about his plight. Whenever he was asked: "How are you doing today?" especially in the hospital, he would say, "Fantastic!"

So Larry was not the person who made it hard for me to be his caregiver, most of the time. It was everybody else.

Every person you come into contact with as a caregiver will likely refuse to talk to you or give you any kind of decent or indecent information without you having to pull out a pre-signed HIPAA form or the almighty Durable Power of Attorney (POA) which we discussed in Chapter One.

As I warned in that chapter, get that POA now or even sooner. So why is this a separate chapter? You need to have some methods of dealing with anyone and everyone because even with your magic POA, you're going to run into roadblocks.

THE DOCTOR

The minute you have the chance TAKE A COPY of your POA to every doctor's office. Do not, under any circumstances, let them keep your original document. If they ask to see the original, and they won't, tell them you'll bring it in another day. Also tell them to put in your loved one's chart, that you are the POA, so that you can talk to anyone in that office.

My brother-in-law had many, many physicians over the years and I made a point to get them a copy of the POA, so that there would never be a question as to who I could talk to, what I could discuss and how I could get things done.

Weirdly, you will rarely have a problem talking to a doctor's billing department. They are so happy to talk to you about who is going to pay the bill and when. Although, I have been told by billing departments that they cannot talk to me without the patient's consent. If I'm with the patient, I put them on the phone to give permission. If I see that this is going to be a long and complicated billing issue I fax them my POA.

THE HOSPITAL

If you live in a small town, like I do, you often end up at the same hospital, especially in emergencies. In an emergency, you don't need to carry that POA around with you, but eventually get that in your loved one's hospital record. Larry was in and out of the hospital many, many times and I would tell them to check their records if they didn't believe me. The POA was there, and I had no time for shenanigans.

Sometimes, my brother-in-law had to be transferred to a different hospital. I would always immediately tell the nurses' station that I was his POA, and if I did not have the document with me, I would get it to them as soon as possible.

Once a POA is in someone's hospital record, it's pretty much there for the duration. This is an actual upside of computers. Because they usually scan these documents into the system, it stays there like toilet paper stuck to your shoe....in a good way....unless and until a new one is put into the system. That's a plus for you as the POA. You can tell them look for my POA in your system. And when they tell you it's not there, tell them to look harder. It's there.

THE BANK

It's important that you understand the distinction between the Durable Healthcare POA and the Durable Financial POA. If these are two different documents, instead of one combined document then you need to make sure you take the correct document with you to the bank. The bank only needs the Durable Financial POA.

In some states, a bank may try and require you to have your loved one sign a POA that is their own form. This used to be the case in Pennsylvania. Thankfully, that is no longer true. The bank must honor your legitimate POA, created by your own lawyer if it meets the requirements of Pennsylvania. I cannot speak to other states. I can tell you that 'in the olden days' on behalf of my clients, I would call the legal department of a bank and speak to their attorneys to have them accept a perfectly legitimate POA drafted and properly executed by my office, and it usually solved the problem.

If you can take your loved one with you to the bank to confirm that this is their POA and their wishes, it will only make your life easier. However, as is often the case, a POA is scrambling to get their loved one's affairs in order when an emergency has occurred or dementia has now set in. Thankfully, you had that POA in place for just such an occasion. Just because you didn't yet get to the bank, the doctor, or anyone else does not mean you aren't prepared! Yay, you!

If a bank or financial institution is giving you trouble, you might have to enlist the services of the attorney who drafted your documents. This will be worth the time, I assure you. Also, if you are using your Mom's attorney, your Mom should be paying the bill out of her assets, if possible. I am not advocating that you go around throwing Mom's money at her problems. But I am saying that if it's necessary for you to obtain expert assistance for your Mom's legal issues, and your Mom has assets, use them for her care. It is no different than Mom paying a copay for her prescription drugs, or at the doctor's office. The law does not expect you to bankroll expenses for Mom's care, and the rest of your family shouldn't expect it either.

THE FINANCIAL ADVISOR

This should be as simple as the bank. Again, don't let the financial advisor tell you that his parent company requires their own document. If need be, you ask to speak to the legal department, or better yet, get your loved one's attorney to call the Financial Advisor and discuss the legitimacy of the POA.

You will meet resistance if your loved one did not tell his/her Financial Advisor in advance that you are the POA. But, if your loved one has these documents in order, and you were not even aware that you had been appointed a POA, the documents rule.

It never hurts to have your loved one's lawyer, doctor, and banker on your team. If you can get them acquainted with you before the proverbial "%$*$# hits the fan," it will be better for all concerned. If you know you are the POA and it looks like you will be doing much more work for your loved one in terms of their personal affairs, get to these important people as soon as possible. If your loved one is still healthy enough to accompany you, take them with you so that the doctor, the bank, and the financial advisor are assured that this meets with your loved one's wishes.

THE HEALTH INSURANCE COMPANY

(the Medigap Insurance Company or the Medicare Part C Insurance Company)

Now it's getting a bit trickier. You can't show up at the insurance company with your elderly mother, go to each department and say, "hey, we're just here to let you know I'm her POA."

You have to become a navigator better than Magellan. You will need to call the customer service department, tell them you want to file a Power of Attorney document with them on behalf of your loved one, and ask them how to do that.

Usually, they will tell you that you can fax a copy or send a copy. I often do both, just to make sure it doesn't get lost in the process. You can go to your local Staples or Office Max and fax a copy to the Insurance Company. While you are there, make a copy or several copies, as you can see you will need them. DO NOT EVER WRITE ON THE ORIGINAL POA.

These are the steps to follow:

1. Make several photocopies of the original POA.
2. Put the original POA back in the folder or envelope you brought to the copy store.
3. Collate each *copy* of the POA.
4. On each *copy* of the POA write the appropriate insurance information as follows:
   a. Put your loved one's Name at the top of each page.
   b. If they use your loved one's Medicare # for ID, write it at the top of each page of the document.
   c. If they use an ID# and/or Group Insurance # Put those numbers at the top of each page.
   d. If they require a Date of Birth put that at the top of each page as well.
   e. Write on the copy, after you have sent it, the date you faxed and/or mailed it. So that when they tell you they don't have it, you can use that date.

Whatever information they requested you provide before mailing or faxing the POA to them, make sure it is on the *COPY.*

DO NOT EVER WRITE ANY ADDITIONAL INFORMATION ON THE ORIGINAL POWER OF ATTORNEY. THIS CAN INVALIDATE YOUR POA.

OTHER INSURANCE COMPANIES (HOMEOWNERS, AUTO, LIFE, LONG-TERM CARE)

All of these insurance companies can legitimately ask for the POA in order to do business with you for your loved one. If you are the POA for someone who has Long Term Care Insurance, I would definitely contact that Long-Term Care Insurer. If you are looking into your crystal ball and see that you are in this for the long haul with your loved one, that insurance company will want a copy of the POA. The earlier you provide that POA to them, the easier it will be to deal with them. Once you need their services you will be glad that you do not need to deal with administrative issues.

As to the rest of the other insurance companies, I would say you decide how and when. It is unlikely that your dad's auto insurance company won't speak to you about paying a bill or cancelling the policy if you've sold the family car.

The whole point here is to make your life as the POA and caregiver as easy as possible before it becomes so complicated you can't breathe. I hope that never happens, but if it does, you will be happy that much of this baloney is off the table.

MEDICARE (not Medicaid…see Chapter Two)

If you need to talk to Medicare about why bills haven't been paid, you need to file your POA documents at a super secret special place. I have included the link to the form at the end of this section. You can find the form at www.medicare.gov under Medicare forms. It is the form CMS 10106 Authorization to Disclose Personal Health Information. It is designed to be signed by the person on Medicare. If you can have your loved one sign, or you are the person on Medicare and can sign it, by all means, do so. You can tell them that you wish this authority to be unending. You can have your loved one sign it now, while they are perfectly capable of handling their own affairs. If you are or are going to be the go to person to make phone calls and inquiries to Medicare now or in the future, file the paper. It's there when you need it. There is also a form to revoke this authority if need be. Do it now and you won't regret it.

If your loved one is no longer able to sign this form, the form can be signed by the POA, and when you send it in to Medicare, you must include a *copy* of the POA as well.

Be aware, that it can take up to two months to process this document. So if you can do this now in anticipation of the future, in the words of Larry (the Cable Guy, not my brother-in-law) "Git Er Done!"

Medicare has a special form for this. This is what it says when you go to Forms under Medicare.gov:

I want to make sure Medicare can give my personal health information to someone other than me (Authorization to Disclose Personal Health Information form/CMS-10106).

This is the form you need to complete:

https://www.cms.gov/Medicare/CMS-Forms/CMS-Forms/Downloads/CMS10106.pdf

SOCIAL SECURITY

Let us continue on our treacherous journey of ways to make the caregiver's life complicated, convoluted and downright crazy.

So you want to talk to Social Security about your mom? Ha! First and foremost, have your mom in the room right next to you, if possible. This is the blessing of cell phones. In the ancient days of practicing law, I would have to go to my grandmother's house and sit with her by the phone to make sure they knew she was in the room with me and could acknowledge her permission for Social Security to speak to me.

At least you can take your phone to wherever Mom and Dad are and start the process from there. Generally, I don't recommend taking Mom to the Social Security Office. But you might just have to do that. If so, make an appointment. You will wait on the phone for 30 or 40 or a billion minutes trying to make the appointment, but the alternative is to go down to the office, take a number and wait your turn, much like the dreaded Department of Motor Vehicles. I will say, I've had some lucky breaks at the Social Security Office, but I live in a small town and we have a small satellite office unlike the county seat. Try and do your business on the phone or make an appointment. None of it will be easy, but you will save time.

And set up an online Social Security account for you and for you loved one. This account gives you access to review your Social Security information, get a new card if you've lost yours and do some other important things. Everyone should set up their own account with Social Security. Just go to www.socialsecurity.gov and follow the instructions. And write down your password. I know you all have a place where you've written down your passwords because I do too!

Why would you need to talk to Social Security?

There are many reasons:

If you are moving your loved one, you are in charge of changing his/her address for Social Security and Medicare. You have to do that on the phone, on line through your personal Social Security account, or in person.

If you want to appeal a Medicare decision, you need an Appointment of Representative form.

If you want to change your loved one's bank account for Direct Deposit, you need Social Security forms and their permission.

Technically, if you are on a bank account with your loved one, you are required to file a document called a Representative Payee Form.

So for all of those reasons, and so many more, you need to let Social Security know you are the POA. And....they don't care.

Every single form they have is required and your POA means nothing to them. What can you do? You can get all the forms, fill them out, and have your loved one sign them. If your loved one is not capable of signing, you can sign as POA and include your document. But the key is that you must use their forms and your POA is merely an adjunct.

Go to their website, it's fun! Well, okay, it's informative www.socialsecurity.com

UNITED STATES DEPARTMENT OF VETERANS AFFAIRS 1-800-827-1000

Most of us refer to this as the VA or the Veterans Administration. The VA has very strict rules about who can help a

Veteran file a claim, appeal a claim or speak on their behalf. Attorneys must be accredited to work with the VA and cannot charge a fee until a claim has been processed.

What you can do is call the phone number up above and tell the customer service representative that you wish to have someone speak on your behalf, if you are the one who is receiving Veteran's benefits. Caregivers must do that first phone call with their loved one so that the loved one can get on the phone and give permission to the VA to speak with you, the caregiver.

In that same conversation, you must ask the VA to send you Form 21-0845. The name of this form is Authorization to Disclose Personal Information to a Third Party. Fill out the document and send it with a copy of your Power of Attorney. The main link for the Veterans Administration is www.va.gov. You can find this form online at the VA website and print it. At this link:

http://www.vba.va.gov/pubs/forms/VBA-21-0845-ARE.pdf

The VA does have an entire section for caregivers as well, with many topics. It is definitely worth looking at.

The problem here is the VA authorization document is structured for you to speak to the VA about a limited incident or time period. I have no idea why they would not have a document just for the submission of a POA. This would make sense, especially in light of the fact that probably 92% of people contacting the VA are caregivers trying to help a loved one. But why would they think of that? I'm pretty sure that every single day, every single customer service representative at the VA is on the phone with a caregiver telling the caregiver that the VA can't talk to them, because they don't have the proper authority.

They use HIPAA as their excuse. HIPAA is supposed to mean the Health Insurance Portability and Accountability Act. It's supposed to protect all of us from having our health information blabbed out to anyone and everyone. However, I'm pretty sure it means:

Ha! Information Possessors Are never going to Assist you.

But once you get that Form 21-0845, you can file it in such a way as to make it seem like you never want the authority to speak to the VA to end. It has worked for me so far, so I suppose there's hope. Try it.

Moral of the Story: Do what you can, as soon as you can, in every single instance, here and now in your life as a caregiver to make sure everyone knows you have the authority to talk about your loved one's health and financial issues. If you do caregiving will seem like a Caribbean vacation. Okay, not that, but better, it will be better.

CHAPTER SIX

HOW TO ASK FOR HELP

Last Wednesday I got the phone call every girl dreams of. Yes, George Clooney invited me to his lake house on the Amalfi Coast! Actually, it was better than that. My Congressman called me.

Since January, I have spent countless hours on the phone and faxing, scanning, emailing and snail-mailing documents to various demons of the Veterans Affairs and Department of Defense hoping against hope that I could stave off a medical insurance disaster for my elderly mom, before it happened.

In the interim, my husband suggested I call our Congressman. He noticed that our Congressman has a position on the Veterans Administration Committee. So, what the heck! Ain't that what we pay these guys for?

I spoke with the ever-so-kind assistant in charge of Veterans' issues. I faxed her all the documentation that I was constantly sending out to the Federalis. And for some odd reason, I just let her do her thing and waited to hear from her, probably because I continued to inundate myself with phone calls and wild goose chases to the VA.

A few days later, the office called to say that the Congressman was able to get my mother registered with the correct medical insurance and problem solved!! Hooray. Happiness, Joy, Exaltation.

Not so fast...................

"That's the good news," she said. Uh oh.

"The only glitch is, your mother has to submit all those incorrectly paid bills, for the last 15 years, to the new insurance within 180 days or it will not be covered and she will be responsible for those medical bills,"

Oh gee whiz, that sounds so easy, like , I don't know, gathering all the pine cones in the forest for the last 15 years and then shoving them up their .... sorry, I got distracted looking for a metaphor.

"But we have eight months!" she exclaimed.

Yay?

Yet, she most assuredly told me that she would assist me in getting all that information from the old insurance company to send to the new one. Mind you, these are both arms of Veterans Affairs insurance. It's not like it is Aetna and United Healthcare. They are both Veterans medical insurance.

But they are not allowed to talk to each other. Only we can talk to them and then transfer information back and forth. I found that out in my 10,000 phone calls between all these quasi-agencies.

But I can live with this. I can do it!

So I want to right here, right now, give a formal thank you to my Congressman, who I did not vote for, but who has restored my faith just a bit in the system. He worked for his constituents, regardless of their party affiliation to solve a real problem in his District. I am grateful for his attention to this problem and for his associate, for tackling this crazy issue in record time.

See, people it can be done. People who don't agree on everything can help one another and get things done. Wow, what a concept.

And it never hurts to laugh while helping....And dream of George Clooney's House on the Amalfi Coast....

This may be the one thing every blessed, kind, giving, under-loved, under-appreciated caregiver just doesn't do. Sometimes because you don't know how to do it, sometimes because you don't feel comfortable doing it, sometimes you don't feel like you deserve to do it. This short chapter is here to help you do it. Ask for help. You have read countless articles, pamphlets and websites about how you need to take care of yourself. This may be the best thing you can do in that category. First, because you need to be the healthiest person in the room and second because any time you have time off, whether it be fifteen minutes or fifteen days, you become a better caregiver.

There's a second reason you need to ask for help, and it's not for you. It's for the person you are asking to help you.

When you tell your son, daughter, sister, brother, mom's best friend…that by not showing up, and me allowing you to do so because I think it's a punishment or burden to help out…what I'm really doing is preventing you from doing a good thing or a mitzvah (as my dear Jewish friends would tell you).

It is my failing as a caregiver that I have not allowed you to take the reins for a moment or an extended period because I think I'm protecting you. But I, the caregiver, am depriving you from these memories, these shared moments with your loved one. I am preventing you from having the knowledge that you did something important, something real and strengthened your relationship with your loved one. Even if your loved one lives another billion years, or only a short period of time, the two of you will have had this special time when you stepped up and shared a difficult time, and you could show them you loved them just by showing up.

So here are a few suggestions and a fun party game for asking for help!

1. HOW TO ASK FOR GENERAL HELP.

Hi _____, it's _____
      (name)   (your name, about time, the call you dreaded)

I was wondering what you are doing_____!
              (pick a day, date, month, year)

I could use _____.
      (help, a break, a drink, Valium)

Do you think you could _____?
(come over, give me an hour, bring wine, let me take a vacation)

How about if you_____ with your _____?
   (help, visit, shop, entertain, stay)   (mother,   father,
                            name any relative)

We could_____
        (socialize, make Margaritas, help each other, give mom
   a bath, walk the dog, let me go out for dinner with my husband)

and then you could_____.
> (spend time with (name relative), feel good about yourself, understand my plight, learn a new recipe for Margaritas.

This should only take about _____.
> (an hour, two hours, a day, a weekend, every Tuesday (add time frame desired)

I would be so grateful if you could_____.
> (take the time, walk a mile in my shoes, remember you love (name relative)

I know that_____ would love to spend time with you
> (I or name relative)

 if only to_____.
(be entertained, let you in on our family secrets, beat you over the head with how hard this is)

Let's make it _____,
> (now, as soon as possible, a regular thing, something we both do)

Because we both_____.
> (love (name relative), hate (name relative), want to inherit, have an obligation, realize it's too much for one person, like to drink Margaritas)

2. HOW TO ASK SOMEONE TO TAKE AN APPOINTMENT FOR YOU.

Who Moved My Teeth?

Hi _____ , it's _____
      (name)   (your name, going to be fun, something special just for you)

I was wondering what you are doing_____!
      (pick date of appointment but throw in other dates of possibility so they can't say they're busy every day).

So_____has an appointment.
      (mom, dad, me, my dog)

I so glad you're_____.
      (not busy, willing to help, retired, have a car, finally got a conscience)

It will only take_____.
      (an hour, two hours, your whole freaking day, someone with a heart)

The appointment is at_____.
      (name of doctor, hospital, DMV, Social Security Office, bank, Veterans Office, hairdresser, church, barber, pharmacy, Chipotle)

You need to be here _____.
    (in the AM, the PM, before rush hour, in time to help me bathe and dress (name relative), before I kill someone)

I'll have_____ ready, but I need you to_____.
    (name relative, coffee, tea, a gift card)   (come early, take loved one to lunch, bring cream)

Don't worry, it's really_____
                       (easy, hard, exhausting, fun and you get lunch
                       with (name relative).

Don't forget to take_____.
                (the insurance card, the co-pay, Depends, money for
lunch, a book)

I'm so_____ and sure you will be_____
   (grateful, happy, relieved, eating chocolate)   (fine, frustrated,
                                      drinking your dinner)

3. HOW TO ASK SOMEONE TO TAKE YOUR LOVED ONE SHOPPING.

Hi _____, it's _____
        (name)   (your name, going to be a fun
                               conversation, your turn)

I was wondering what you are doing_____!
                     (pick a day, date, month,year)

Our_____
 (name of loved one, plan, relationship)

needs to_____.
(grocery shop, go to the drug store, include you, improve)

Since you_____,
(are also related to (name relative), are not busy, have time to blow your
      nose)

can you _____

      (take (name loved one) to the store, the zoo, for a massage, please help)

I've made a _____

      (list, easy route, cake for later, vacation plans)

and that will make _____

      (your life easier, your life harder, my life better, for a fun story!)

You can_____

    (pick up (name of loved one), come early, do this every week, bring snacks)

at_____

  (her house, my house, (name time), every opportunity)

I am so_____

      (grateful for your help, surprised you're still listening, looking forward to this break)

Let me know_____

      (how it goes, what I can do for you, if you will ever answer the phone again)

Thanks for_____

      (helping, answering the phone, taking a turn, making my day)

Now that you've asked for help, you can indeed take some time to care for yourself. Let's see if that's a possibility.

CHAPTER SEVEN

THE SEVEN DWARFS OF HIDDEN SYMPTOMS

Or Why is My Loved One Dopey, Grumpy, Sneezy, Sleepy, Bashful, not Happy and where is the Doc?

I have done something very naughty. I must even go so far as to admit I have done it on purpose. You will probably not agree with my decision, but in the end, was I right? If you've read any of my blogs....you know the answer to that.

Being a caregiver puts you in the 'decider' seat more times than you care to admit. And sometimes you don't want to be George W. Bush....you WANT someone else to be the decider. But alas, you're it. You are the caregiver.

The hired caregivers, who do all the hard stuff, the bathing, the dressing, the cleaning up, keeping the list of needed items gladly call on the decider when well, when decisions must be made.

So, I get a call from Tracy, head honcho hired caregiver:

"Cathy, your brother-in-law, is acting weird."

"Weirder than usual," I say, hoping that this is just happy conversation, knowing all the while that I am in for a project.

"No, not usual weird---- cranky, mean and kind of 'out of it' weird", she says weirdly, knowing that I KNOW she wouldn't call me unless there was a problem to be solved.

"Hmmmm, that sounds like, 'you-know-what', doesn't it," I say with regret.

"Yup," she says, " a UTI" (everyone's worst caregiving enemy...the urinary tract infection). "He's weird, he's ornery and his urine looks a little tinged with brown. So that's not good."

"Okey dokey," I say with false upbeat. "I'll call the visiting nurse he has right now and get her to call the doctor."

I have to go this convoluted way because I have no medical authority to call the doctor and beg for an antibiotic.

"Hello, Visiting Nurse? I want to ensnare you to do my dirty work," Okay, I really don't say that.

"Hello, Visiting Nurse? I got a call from the caregivers and they think Larry's behavior and his urine suggest a UTI. I would be ever so grateful if you would call his doctor for a prescription because it's Friday, I can't get him to the doctor for at least three days, and if it gets too far gone, he usually ends up in the hospital."

"Ok," says the Visiting Nurse, "I will call this morning and get back to you."

By 4 o'clock, I haven't heard from anyone. So I call the pharmacist to see if there is a prescription waiting. No, of course not. So I call the doctor's office.

"Hi, I'm calling because I know the Visiting Nurse called and the pharmacy has no prescription."

"Yes, we see that the Visiting Nurse called this morning, and it's in the doctor's inbox to process."

"I understand that the doctor is busy," I say patiently (really I do) but it's Friday afternoon, and these UTI's can be very dangerous for this guy....so if you could just see if he can get it processed tonight......"

"I'll put a reminder on it," says the receptionist.

So, of course, at 8:30 that night the Visiting Nurse calls to tell me they called in a prescription, with the caveat that the nurse would take a urine sample and have it to the lab BEFORE we give him the medicine, just to make sure.

So she gets the sample. I get the meds into him the next morning, and two days later they call and tell me the sample is negative.

And here's where I'm naughty.

Years ago, when my kids were toddlers, they would suffer from chronic ear infections. I would see it coming, take them to the pediatrician, no red ears would appear in the otoscope, and the pediatrician would send me home. A day or two later, I would be right back in that office with a kid with DOUBLE ear infections, because the symptoms were obvious to me, but not yet to the otoscope. And pretty much, every time, Dr. MOM was right.

Soooooo.........I just kept on giving that antibiotic to my brother-in-law since his symptoms were so obvious to all of us caregivers, he gets really, really, REALLY sick if he gets an untreated UTI, and I just was willing to go for it. I am the decider.

I know. I know. Too many antibiotics, too much MERSA, too many super bugs. I know.

But here's the kicker. THREE DAYS LATER, the doctor's office calls me and says.

"Well, you know the test was negative for an infection, but all the other markers were questionable, and so we thought an infection was on the horizon, so just finish the antibiotic as given.

Yup, DR. MOM!!!!

A. UTI'S OR UNBEARABLE TRAUMA IN CAREGIVING AND OTHER HIDDEN SYMPTOMS

Why do we need a whole chapter on hidden symptoms? In my life as a caregiver, I truly wish someone had given me this information about hidden symptoms Because this one little, seemingly harmless bodily infection or common diseases with their hidden symptoms can wreak more havoc in a caregiver's life than a tsunami in the Pacific Ocean.

What is a UTI and why is it so problematic?

A UTI is a urinary tract infection. But a Urinary Tract Infection is some kind of infection that gets into the system of seemingly every single old or frail person who is dealing with health issues. Next to pneumonia, it is the most common infection in those with fragile health. It's probably just as common in caregivers but much less reported, as they too are suffering from compromised health through stress.

Elderly people with serious urinary tract infections don't exhibit the hallmark sign of fever because their immune system is unable to mount a response to infection due to the effects of aging. In fact, elders often don't exhibit any of the common symptoms – or don't express them to their caregivers.

So let's deal with your loved one who is suffering from a UTI.

If you are new to the world of UTI's you will think this chapter is a silly waste of your time. You will think that you will know, or your loved one's doctor or hired caregiver will know when a UTI has stricken. That most assuredly is never the case. The symptoms are devious. They often don't appear. When the symptoms do appear, it can be confused with another illness. But the worst problem by far with UTI symptoms is that doctors, hired caregivers, other relatives and even the one with the UTI often think that there's not a damn thing wrong.

This is how it goes down:

Caregiver: Dad, you don't seem yourself today.

Dad: I'm fine. What are you talking about? I'm so sick of you trying to make it sound like I'm sick when I'm perfectly fine.

Caregiver: Okay, Dad. You just seem a little cranky and out of sorts. Your hired caregiver said you wouldn't take your meds today. She also said you weren't eating or drinking very much.

Dad: Oh, what does she know?! I just didn't feel like it. Leave me be.

At this point you are wondering where your sweet dad went. He can have his moments but he always takes his meds without fail, and he's never nasty to the help.

That night at 11:00 P.M. (because no one ever gets sick at 10:00 A.M. or on a lazy Sunday afternoon) you are called by the assisted living facility that your Dad has been rushed to the ER with a high fever and acting like a demented spawn of Satan.

Your loved one has never acted this way. And so it begins.

This scenario begins to repeat itself—once a year, once a quarter, once a month and sometimes more often than that.

The primary caregiver has learned the pattern. Whenever her loved one starts to act out of character, cranky, listless, uncooperative, not eating or drinking, it could be any one of these things or a combination of these things. Invariably, it's a UTI.

Because these symptoms are not typical of a bodily infection, there's no fever, no pain in urination, no other outward signs of sickness, the elder or frail health person is not given any credence. Worse, is the fact that the caregiver is considered an alarmist, or over-protective.

As my story related, I remember a time when my toddler used to get serious ear infections on a pretty regular basis. She rarely got a fever, and never tugged at her ear. She just became the three-year-old from hell. Since 'terrible-twos' have nothing on 'terroristic-threes,' I was under the impression that I had to deal with bad behavior as any young mother should. Eventually, I understood that when my sweet, little muffin turned into toddzilla with no warning, it was usually an ear infection.

I can't tell you the number of times I went to the nurse practitioner insisting that my adorable first born had an ear infection and not a death wish. I can tell you the number of times I allowed them to turn me away telling me there wasn't a thing wrong with her. Two. I let them get away with it twice and then I insisted they check BOTH her ears and every time at least one of them was on the way to earmania.

That's the foundation I had for UTIs as a caregiver.

When I figured out with my brother-in-law that his behavior was more indicative of a UTI than any medical symptoms, I was on high alert as soon as things appeared fishy.

Here are some things I noticed:

1. He would get very cranky. (He was a curmudgeon, but he took it to a new level)

He would be mean to everyone. Not just the people he didn't like, the cleaning lady, the hired caregivers, the podiatrist who came to cut his toenails, the teenage waitresses who worked in the dining hall after school, even people on TV who couldn't hear a word he said. If he was 'starting to go down', as I began to call it, he would yell at Rachael Ray like she was sitting next to him for making a dish he despised.

Normally my brother-in-law loved the kids who worked in the dining hall. He was a favorite of the caregivers because he was young and interesting and had no dementia. He was a great patient in every sense of the word with medical providers. He took his meds, he joked with ambulance drivers, he cooperated with many an undignified poking and prodding. So when all this changed on a dime, I knew there was trouble in paradise.

2. He would not take his medication.

Now sometimes he would be nice about this, but he would never refuse meds if he was feeling well. Refusal to take meds was always a big red flag. I instructed his caregivers to alert me if he started this behavior. It was a signal to take action.

3. He would not drink.

Sometimes he would eat and not drink. Since he loved hot tea, iced tea, and juice, I knew something was up when he went on a fluid strike. He might still eat, but not drink. Pay attention to this. As caregivers know, stopping liquids is a slippery slope to the ER. If I could make my caregivees continue to do one thing when they start feeling bad, it's drink water, or almost anything for that matter. One can never underestimate the value of hydration. If they have to go to the ER and all liquids are banned until they can figure out what's going on, your loved one would be happy to be hydrated. You might want to drink to…water, I mean water (save the wine for when you get home from the hospital).

4. He stopped eating.

This seems obvious, but everyone has days where they are not hungry. Picky eating or someone who never ate much is not the same as stopping food. Just be aware a day or a day-and-a-half of truly not eating is bad news.

5. He would start talking nonsense.

My brother-in-law never had dementia. He would suddenly start acting confused. He would utter nonsense. He wouldn't understand what was being asked of him. If your loved one, who may sometimes be confused or take a lot of thinking time, gets to this new level of confusion and it escalates, even just a little bit, pay attention. This can be a UTI and a trip to the ER in no time

6. He would be restless.

I would rarely get phone calls from my brother-in-law. On days when he would call me several times, or have his caregivers call me, my UTI radar would start going off like a cannon in the William Tell overture.

7. He would refuse to get dressed or hate his outfit.

This was such a blatant crazy move that we all knew he was 'going down.' He was wheelchair bound, so no clothes to go to the dining room was not an option. It was not even an option in his room where his caregivers would come when he wasn't feeling well to help him eat in his room. He was not a member of the fashion police. So although he might prefer a short-sleeved shirt to a long-sleeved shirt, that was where his chic requirements usually ended. If he hated a color or a fabric and made a huge deal about that, yeah, something is going on inside that urinary tract.

8. He slept way too much.

He would have an occasional night where he wouldn't sleep well. That had a rare effect on his personality or behavior. He could take a nap during the day and usually took two. So a day where he was napping a couple times in the day wasn't news. But if no one could wake him in the morning or from a nap, or there was a whole day of napping and pretty much nothing else, I called the doctor.

Every one of these symptoms was considered 'nothing' from the doctor, the nurse practitioner, the ambulance crew and the ER staff, until they did a urinalysis. And those UTIs were rampant, that bacteria was all over the place. Eventually, UTIs became a serious downfall in my brother-in-law's health.

9. He would fall down or drop things

Dropping things when you have Multiple Sclerosis in an advanced stage is not unusual. Before he was wheelchair bound, my brother-in-law would stumble occasionally but, again he had Multiple Sclerosis. However, as his primary caregiver who spent oodles of time with him, I began to see what was the new 'normal' and what was out of character. There were certain ways he would lose balance that might be different. And without a doubt, these symptoms of a UTI were usually a conglomeration not just one missed symptom.

Caregivers need to trust their instincts that the one they are caring for is a little off. This just happened to me last week. My friend, who suffered a Traumatic Brain Injury (TBI) several years ago, went out to lunch with us. She was just not herself. During her recovery several of us became her caregivers. It's been a few years, but TBIs have far-reaching affects usually for a lifetime. And although I noticed she was a bit "off" that day, I failed to mention it. The next day she was in the ER with a serious downturn in her hemoglobin due to blood loss from an undetected ulcer. Still, after 25 years of caregiving for so many people, I did not trust my instincts.

Because UTIs are one of the most common undetected, under-diagnosed conditions in the elderly and infirm, especially since the symptoms imitate dementia-like behavior, all caregivers need to be aware of these hidden symptoms. As caregivers, or even as one who is taking care of one's own health, you must forcefully request that you or your loved one be tested for a urinary tract infection.

Hidden symptoms can be the culprit in many other illnesses that plague the elderly or infirm.

B. HIDDEN SYMPTOMS OF DEHYDRATION

Most people don't drink enough water. Elders are probably even worse. Ever since we were told to drink 8 glasses of water a day, we've rebelled. Oh, how I hate when the water police are right. We need to drink more water because the consequences can be deadly. No, really.

One year on a lovely family vacation to the beach, my mother-in-law started to act oddly. First, she wouldn't eat. My mother-in-law never had one of those days. Her appetite was unparalleled. She watched her weight for many years. When we had to change her diet due to a diabetes scare, she was compliant. But she never stopped eating. So when she wouldn't eat it raised all kinds of alarms. Second, she wasn't engaging with her grandchildren. By then they were teenagers and she had a devilish relationship with them where they would tease each other constantly. But on this day, on vacation, she was not interested. Third, her sister-in-law got mad at her because she wouldn't watch the U.S. Open with her. I told my husband to get the keys, we were taking my mother-in-law to the Emergency Room.

Her blood pressure was in the basement, and she religiously took her medication to keep it down. Her blood sugar was through the roof, and she was severely dehydrated. It's likely that the dehydration started all these problems, because on top of not drinking much water, my mother-in-law loved coffee, a diuretic…a substance that makes you naturally dehydrate.

Thirst was the obvious warning. But here are some things we didn't notice right away.

A. Chart of Hidden Symptoms of Dehydration

- Cramping or muscle aches or spasms

- Headaches

- Sleepiness or Irritability

- Weakness or Not Feeling Well

- Acting oddly, not like herself

- Bloated stomach

- Dry eyes or no tears

- Low blood pressure, especially if they usually have high blood pressure

Dehydration seems so mundane, but especially in this population, it can have dire consequences. My mother-in-law was in the hospital for a week getting her health back to normal. Primary caregivers and hired caregivers can take the lead and have that water bottle as a constant companion for the caregivee as well as for themselves.

C. **HIDDEN SYMPTOMS OF RESPIRATORY INFECTIONS**

Respiratory ailments in the elderly are as common as gray hairs. Yet, these too, can go undiagnosed for periods of time because of misunderstood symptoms. Even we caregivers are quick to judge our loved one's behaviors as just being old or chronically ill. All too often, when we are back in that ER for what seems like the hundredth time, we realize the symptoms were there for us to see.

Many elderly patients are diagnosed with COPD (chronic obstructive pulmonary disease). In fact, many are misdiagnosed with this disease where it may be asthma, obesity, emphysema or a myriad of other problems. All of these diagnoses can lead to acute respiratory problems. Even without any of these diagnoses, elders and chronically ill people are already at risk for respiratory illness or failure.

So here are some signs to note when respiratory illness or failure can be imminent

- Curtailing activities

- Depression

- Anxiety

- Confusion

- Coughing

- Feeling Weak

- Chills

- Shortness of Breath

- Fever

The problem with waiting too long to notice a respiratory illness is that it can lead to the dire consequences of pneumonia, and as caregivers, we all know the slippery slope of that problem. Being on the lookout for respiratory issues is not being an alarmist. Don't let anyone tell you it is.

D. HIDDEN SYMPTOMS OF DRUG AND ALCOHOL ABUSE

This is a boozy doozy. A quick search of this topic on the Internet indicates the lack of research or even medical questioning or reporting of drug and alcohol abuse in the elderly.

No, your grandma is not going down to the railroad tracks to score some heroin. And in fact, this is probably less about your grandma, than it is about you. Research is showing that the Baby Boomers are the ones who are concentrating their efforts to stay free of stress by over-indulging in alcohol and prescription drugs, and even marijuana because that was a big drug of choice as we were growing up.

So this message is probably more for you, the caregiver, than your mom or dad who is limited to two drinks at cocktail hour in the fancy dancy assisted living facility they saved so diligently to afford.

The guidelines currently out there for healthy drinking in the aged is no more than one drink per day. Now even I will tell you that with my generation that guideline is absurd. If I am at any social gathering with friends and family and I do decide to have a drink, it's usually at least 2 glasses of wine. Yeah, that's 'a' drink. I think that's true in most social lexicons. But I don't drink every day, not even every week sometimes.

However, as unrealistic as one drink per day seems, this is about hidden symptoms. Interestingly, unscientific surveys have shown that most caregivers and families of caregivers take the attitude AS caregivers that, "hey, this is Grandpa's last hurrah, if he wants to drink Jim Beam every night, why not? If he needs 2 Percocets every day to deal with his aches and pains, who cares?"

And I'm largely in that school. The problem is when drugs and alcohol make us or our loved ones dangerous to ourselves or others.

- Are we increasing the likelihood of a fall? We all know the dire consequences of that.

- Are we really improving the quality of their life or are they so depressed this is only making it worse? Because, you do know alcohol is a depressant, right?

- Are we truly making them more comfortable every day or are we multiplying their problems with yet another health issue that makes them feel like crap, constipates them, makes them shaky, makes them angry, or makes them miserable to be around?

- Are we depriving them of good food, fresh air, exercise, good hydration, all of which would put them in a better mood and perhaps better health just so they can have the perceived comfort of being in a fog?

And how does this apply to you, my dear caregiver? Are you putting yourself at risk by using alcohol and drugs to maintain your sanity and composure during this very difficult time? If so, is it really helping? Is this what you think 'taking care of yourself' has to look like?

I'm so in favor of a good stiff drink or a few glasses of wine every once in a while. Caregiving is hard. But the hidden symptoms of alcohol and drug abuse tell the real story about why this is not a good idea for your elder or for you:

- Loss of interest in activities
- Memory problems
- Falls and bruises
- Irritability often about pain killers and alcohol
- Loss of appetite
- Cognitive changes, inability to focus
- Irrational behavior
- Failure to bathe and dress properly
- Profound negativity
- Depression

THE THREE DEADLY D'S

What's blatantly interesting about all these hidden symptoms is many of them are recurring. And many of these hidden symptoms are all often misdiagnosed solely as the three deadly D's: Dementia, Diabetes and Depression.

If the physician keeps telling you that any of these three are the sole problem of your loved one's chronic or acute illness, and you see a change, don't buy it. Insist on tests for whatever you think might be going on. You may save yourself and your loved one a longer hospital stay, a lot less pain, and perhaps even return them to better health much more quickly than expected.

CHAPTER EIGHT

FOR GOD'S SAKE STOP PAYING THOSE MEDICAL BILLS!

I have told my mother, mother-in-law, aunts, uncles, disabled brother-in-law, cousins and pretty much anyone who would listen, that JUST BECAUSE YOU GET A BILL FROM A DOCTOR OR MEDICAL PROVIDER, DOESN'T MEAN YOU HAVE TO PAY IT. As you can imagine from the capital letters, this advice often falls on deaf ears. (Why would I, who practices elder law and has been a caregiver for sick people for over 25 years know anything about this?!!) So the unsuspecting relative, friend, client, pays the bill and then brings it to my attention. Of course, this sends me into a tizzy. Yes, I said tizzy. I rant and rave and get on the phone with the offending billing department, which I know, will be receiving proper payment from insurance.

One such scenario went like this:

"Hello? You sent my mother-in-law a bill, and her insurance has paid you already."

"One moment please. Do you have the account number? The date of service? Her insurance card number? Her other insurance card number? Her date of birth? Her astrological sign?"(Okay they didn't ask for that, but if they did would you really be surprised?)

"Well, yes I see that she has other insurance, but you will have to get a new bill from her doctor showing this, that and the other thing to clear this up."

So I call the doctor. And they are very nice, and more than willing to send me a new bill showing this, that and the other thing for proper credit so that I can get my mother-in-law's $62 returned to her. But the desk clerk leaves me with one thought:

"Good luck getting your mom's $62 back, that almost never happens."

"Oh," I say, "you don't know me."

In three weeks, a $62 check comes to my mother-in-law, who insists on splitting it with me because of the fine legal work she has witnessed. But here's the thing. I would do that again and again for $1 for every elderly person who is paying these bills they shouldn't pay. Many are living on a fixed income, and their insurance does, in fact reimburse the doctor, but the patient doesn't know that and often never sees their money come back to them. Truth be told I might make my first million splitting those bills!

I know, I know. This runs counter to everything you have ever learned if you are a fine upstanding citizen. But trust me, for a while at least, do not pay every damn medical bill that comes into your mailbox.

These are the reasons why:

1. **EVERY STATEMENT IS NOT A BILL**

   Medicare has actually improved this somewhat and so have some of your medical providers. You will get a statement that says "THIS IS NOT A BILL." The statement will itemize every single charge from the hospital, physician, physical therapist or any other medical provider. Then there will be some part of the statement that may show how much has been submitted to insurance, if insurance has paid or how long ago it was submitted.

   The most important thing here is that it says:

   THIS IS NOT A BILL

   Believe it. Believe them. Trust me. When a medical provider is owed money and they are not getting it, they will be relentless until they do. But inevitably your insurance will pay some, if not all, of that medical bill. This goes for caregivers, for their loved ones AND for themselves. If you, the caregiver, are going to your own doctor, DO NOT PAY THAT BILL, until you are absolutely certain that you owe that bill. Every insurance company, whether they are Medicare or not, takes time to process claims. But medical providers hire billing departments and they send out those bills as soon as they are incurred. Make certain all your insurances have paid what they are supposed to pay before you open your checkbook.

2. EVERY BILL THEY SAY YOU OWE IS SUSPECT

After insurance has processed, you will get a bill and it may show some payments from Medicare or no payments from Medicare and it will indicate a balance due. This does not mean you jump up, run to your checkbook, and put a stamp on that return envelope.

This just happened to me last week.

A received a bill from the hospital for my deceased brother-in-law. The bill was $4500. As his former Power of Attorney and now his Executor, I was very familiar with his medical insurance. After months and months of hospital care, I was certain that he satisfied all deductibles and probably all of his co-pays. So an astronomical bill for $4500 was just wrong.

I called the billing department which is several states away from our local hospital, so I couldn't even go in there and talk to anyone, and asked them what this unitemized bill with no date of service on it was actually for?

The answer: "Oh we just re-submitted that to Medicare, you can just ignore it."

See? I know many of you would have drained your checking account to get that bill paid immediately. DON'T DO IT.

If you have any suspicions at all, if you think the bill is too high, if you just don't like the way a bill looks, if there is no date of service or any indication of the services rendered for that bill, make a phone call. Do this:

    a. Call the Medical Provider First

- Ask them what the bill is for.

- Ask them for the date of service.

- Ask them if they have received any payments on the bill.

- Ask them if they submitted it to insurance.

- Ask them WHICH insurance they submitted the bill to.

- Ask them if they have all your insurance information, especially if you have a Medigap policy in addition to your Medicare policy. Often that very important piece of the puzzle is missing and they have failed to submit to Medigap or inform Medicare that you have a Medigap policy.

b. Call your Insurer

You can call Medicare if you need to at 1-800-Medicare (1-800-633-4227). But I would only call them if Medicare hasn't paid and you are certain that your medical provider already sent the claim to Medicare and Medicare processed it. If Medicare hasn't paid and you don't understand why, then by all means call them.

Tip: Try calling Medicare late in the afternoon, or on Friday afternoon. These times usually had less wait time for me.

You should also call your Medigap policy holder. This is any one of those insurance companies that you have purchased a policy from as added benefits to your Medicare coverage, for example, United Healthcare, Blue Cross/Blue Shield, Humana, AARP or any of the dozens of others that may be your health insurance over and above your Medicare.

And don't forget you may be a Medicare Part C person who has purchased a Medicare Advantage Program which is like a Medicare and Medigap rolled into one (sort of). That could be Aetna or Humana or many others as well.

Just call them if a bill looks wrong to you, you don't understand it, you think there is a mistake, or you just don't want to pay it.

Remember that $4500 bill I received from the hospital? Three weeks later I received another bill from the same hospital showing that my brother-in-law now owed $520. Again, I picked up the phone and called the far-away collection agency.

Me: So, now I have a bill for $520 instead of $4500?

Collection Person: Yes ma'am, that's correct. (they're very polite in the south)

Me: Did you submit that to my Medigap Insurance since I gave you that information the last time I called you?

Collection Person: No ma'am. I do not believe we have that information. Let me see…..hmmm. Yes, I see that. No ma'am we did not submit that, we will do that now. You can just ignore that bill for $520.

This happened to you again, you say? Yes, again and again and again.

I have told countless senior citizens and their caregivers, Please, for the love of God, do not pay every medical bill that lands in your mailbox. Make certain it is legitimate and all your insurance coverages that you pay for have been implemented. Otherwise, you are paying twice. You're paying your premium and then you're paying a bill that your insurance is supposed to be paying. Most seniors cannot afford that, and if they can, well then they should give it to their underappreciated, underpaid caregivers.

3. IN NETWORK VS. OUT-OF-NETWORK MEDICAL PROVIDERS

The cost of the difference between using an in-network vs. an out-of-network provider can be astronomical. If you make a conscious choice to go to a medical provider who is out-of-network because you trust them, they are the best in their field, nobody does what they do, then I say go for it. I use out-of-network providers occasionally for what I think are good medical reasons. And I pay a price for that. My insurance takes a deep cut. I have a very large deductible for using out-of-network providers. So I take it very seriously before I decide to go to one of these providers.

But if you or your loved one has been going to your doctor, hospital, therapist, for years and they change from an in-network provider to an out-of-network provider, and they don't tell you, I would not pay the difference in that bill. This isn't a legal issue it's a moral one. You or your loved one has been a patient there and you deserve respect. Every time you check in to a medical provider's office or place of business they ask for your medical insurance. They know if they are participating with your carrier or not and it is their responsibility to tell you that, especially if you are a long term patient and they have changed their policies.

And if a hospital, who is in-network, sets you up with out-of-network doctors, I would argue that as well. As a patient in a hospital you cannot possibly ask every medical person coming in your room if they are in-network. Not to mention that you are sick....which is why you are in a hospital. Moreover, your caregiver cannot be expected to monitor that kind of behavior 24-7. They can't be with you 24 hours a day in a hospital, they shouldn't have to be, as you are supposed to be in good hands, and your caregiver will also not be interrogating each and every person on the hospital medical team to see if they are in-network.

Don't pay those bills, tell them you were not consulted as to whether an out-of-network provider would be allowed, and you will only pay them what an in-network payment would be, which is likely what your insurance already sent them.

You have the right to stand up for being treated fairly. You have just as much right to be actionable against fraud as Medicare does. And to take advantage of our sick, and our elderly in cases such as this is unconscionable. I feel certain that most of the time those bills will go away, as they should.

As to other bills that are not medical. If you have any question about a bill, call and ask. This is true of your car, your plumbing, your groceries, your pet groomer. My mother-in-law used to check her grocery bill at home every week. I will admit, it drove me nuts, but she found errors in her favor all the time. I took my car to repair the brake light. The next day my car warning light went on that my brake light was out. They fixed it again…yeah, I wasn't paying for that twice. Be an advocate for your mom, your dad, your caregivee, for yourself. And while you're at it…try to find the humor in all of this. There's probably a good belly laugh in there somewhere!

CHAPTER NINE

PATIENCE IS A VIRTUE.

Have you ever had the experience as a caregiver (or even a co-worker) where you've been taking care of someone and they are clearly forgetting things and allowing you to have all the responsibility and power? Basically, they are done. They don't want to engage in any way that is challenging or difficult. And okay, fine. You deal. And then this happens:

"You are going home tomorrow from the nursing home to your own apartment," you say to your brother-in-law, with ever so much enthusiasm because he has been waiting for this day for 5 months.

"I know, but I thought I was going home Tuesday."

"Umm...you are....tomorrow is Tuesday."

"Oh, yeah." Brother-in-law laughs at his own silliness. Then he says, "and it's time to sign up for Medicare, right? It's open enrollment. And we were going to look at all the options to make sure I had the best plan. Did you do that yet?"

This is where I go through these thoughts:

I want to kill you.

Who are you and where is my brother-in-law?

When in the last 7 years have you even said the words, "open enrollment?"

I take a deep, cleansing breath, and say, "Sure, we can work on that when you get home."

"Because your sister and her husband worked at the same employer as I did and they are on the same retirement insurance. He had a heart transplant, so he's no healthier than me, " says the guy who refused to do his physical therapy just so he can hold a cup without spilling it.

Sometimes I want to run away from home.

No worries. I will read the 500 page booklets from Medicare and your employer retiree plan and we will end up doing the same thing we have done for the last three years because the plans in your retirement only have one option with unlimited lifetime benefits. And you've probably used over a million dollars already. And you're young, very young. Sick, but young. That's what I think, but what I say is:

"Okay we will go over that, we have a few weeks yet."

"Okay, just wanted to make sure you were on top of it. Now did I have lunch yet? Why is that picture on the wall crooked? I don't think anyone changed the clock to daylight savings time."

Please God, help me stay more patient, be more patient.

If anyone could take a magic pill while caregiving, it would be the 'patience' pill. During my caregiving with the elderly and infirm, patience was not my strong suit. And then I created a survey and one of the most glaring responses was…"if only I had had more patience."

60 Ways to Be More Patient

1. Count to 10.
Not new, you know the drill, but have you tried it lately?

2. Change the Subject.
   Do you really need to keep harping on that?

3. Walk out of the room and come back.
   It's like 'count to 10' but different. Go away.

4. Wash your hands.
   Just try it.

5. Put on Chapstick.
   By the time you find it in your purse or pocket, you will have changed your attitude.

6. Say a prayer.
   Preferably a long one, like the "Our Father" or whatever your training allows, even if you make it up, make it last and while you're at it, ask for patience.

7. Drink a large glass of water.
   The whole thing, chug it. You know you're not drinking enough water, anyway.

8. Put on some music.
   Not the tv, music, and music your loved one likes would be good. Just sayin'.

9. Read something aloud from a book, the newspaper, or texts from your phone.
   I'm sure you have some reading material somewhere that would be entertaining to both of you.

10. Change what you're doing.

If you're trying to get Mom dressed to go out, get in the car, or eat her breakfast. Pretend you're not. Stop. See if you can go back to it in just 5 long minutes.

11. Take a shower.
    If you're in your own house, this is a good idea. If you're on the phone with your dad, tell him you will call him right back, you need to take a shower, and do it. Take that shower.

12. Take a bath.
    It's like take a shower, but better, if you have the time. And use bubbles, or lavender oil, or some fancy bath stuff you brought home from a hotel three years ago.

13. Make them take a shower or a bath.
    Timing is everything. This may, in fact, be the time to get them in the tub. When my first baby came along, my sister told me, "if you're baby is distressed, put them in water." I was pretty sure she didn't mean drown them, she meant bathe them, it changed their attitude or yours, but somebody was acting differently.

14. Put gum in your mouth.
    Chewing and yelling are hard. Put 5 pieces in there if you have to. Consider returning to your youth and carrying bubblegum in your pocket. Hard to blow bubbles while losing your cool.

15. Blow bubbles
    You can get these at the dollar store. And a bunch of other things that might entertain you or your loved one. Fifteen minutes in the dollar store might end up bringing hours of patience and fun!

16. Jump!

Not out the window. Either with that jump rope you bought in the dollar store, or just do some jumping jacks. I'm good for about five. I look ridiculous and get winded way too quickly. This was not an activity I shared with my loved one, but they sure liked watching me.

17. Tell a joke.

I like to salt and pepper life with humor. You already figured that out. But I do have a list of jokes I keep handy. I should go buy a joke book, and so should you. Everyone around you, including your loved one has not lost his/her sense of humor. Try it. Even if you're bad at it, that in itself, might be funny.

18. Apologize.

Never hurts to say you're sorry, especially if you are. And face it, sometimes you should be.

19. Get out your iPhone.

Now we all know there's a billion things to do on there. But don't get too crazy, you do need to pay attention!

20. Take a picture.

You know that iPhone you just took out? Take some selfies with your loved one. Some of the selfies I have of my brother-in-law with me while he was in the hospital for the hundredth time, are my favorite pictures in my phone. They make me happy. We were just playing around and put aside all the hospital drama.

21. Order food.

If you live in a place where you can order out and they will deliver, go for it. When was the last time your loved one had a pizza?

22. Eat food.
Bring something fun and eat it, together.

23. Turn off the television.
As I said earlier, the 24/7 television would drive me crazy. The constant background noise was overwhelming. Sometimes stopping the noise is calming.

24. Spray perfume.
It never hurts to make it smell good wherever you are. Maybe bring perfume or cologne for your loved one. Maybe they want to smell good!

25. Comb someone's hair.
I used to love combing my little girls' hair. What feels better than going to the hairdresser and having them wash and comb out your hair? It stops the escalation of an argument. Just stop talking, pick up the comb or brush and take a few minutes.

26. Put lotion on you or your loved one.
Lotion just on someone's hands feels nice. And one of the greatest losses is the loss of touch in the elderly and disabled. Touch someone. Hold their hands while you put lotion on them.

27. Clean out a drawer.
Everyone has one of those drawers. Getting rid of stuff is very cathartic.

28. Go through family photos.
This was so fun. I would either do it with my phone or bring old packets of photos and just talk about them with my loved one.

Sometimes I left the photos there, so that next time when I was frustrated I would have a go to activity.

29. Pay bills.
You're probably doing this anyway. Maybe if you leave it in the caregiving time and not add it to your personal time, it will be better. Maybe. Just a thought.

30. Wipe down the kitchen.
Just grab a rag and start wiping things. It feels cleansing.

31. Clean the windows.
This is an annual event in my house. So there's always a window that could use some good ol' Windex. And you know how miraculous Windex is.

32. Dust.
Similar to wiping up the kitchen but without getting your hands wet. Plus, it has an added bonus of letting you organize and throw things away.

33. Tell a story.
Go back in to the archives of your mind. You and your loved one likely share a long history. There has to be some funny moments in there. Or tell them what happened in your day a week ago that has nothing to do with caregiving.

34. Show them a YouTube video.
There are so many choices here, funny, interesting, musical, inspiring, silly, thought-provoking, cats. You and your loved one can get lost in YouTube. When things get frustrating, break out that device and say, "Hey, look at this!"

35. Hold hands and pray.
    There's all kind of prayer. Holding hands alone can be a prayer.

36. Dance.
    Okay, you might be like Elaine from Seinfeld and your loved one might not even be able to dance. You do know that dancing is a good thing? Otherwise how would Zumba be such a phenomenon?

37. Cook.
    If the situation allows for this or if you just need to go away and go home, cooking something nice for yourself or your family can be completely mind-altering. If this creates more stress for you, then let it go. For some of us, being creative in the kitchen, or just the chopping and dicing refocuses our attention.

38. Bake.
    This is better than cooking because there are cookies and cake and pie when you're done.

39. Color in a coloring book
    How great is it that we now live in a world where there are Adult Coloring Books? Buy one for you and one for your loved one. Get out those colored pencils, crayons, and markers and just sit and color. No need for conversation.

40. Go out to the garden and pick flowers
    I confess, I have gone out to the garden of the nursing home and the assisted living and picked some of their flowers. Just to get out of the building, get some sunshine and bring a bit of that sunshine back into my loved one's room.

41. Get in the car and go for a ride to nowhere

And then get ice cream.

42. Bring a baby, a toy, a game, a doll

Remember that trip to the dollar store? This is where you go into the stash you created and bring something. But if you have a grandchild or two, it would be great to bring them. Kids change the game, attention is re-focused. You could always borrow your friend's grandchild…that young mom may be happy for the break, too!

43. Sing!

Remember "She'll Be Comin' Round the Mountain?", how about "Home on the Range?" I'll bet you and your loved one have more songs in common than you know. You could teach them a new song, like "Happy' from Pharrell.

44. Let them make a decision.

This is a big one. Even if it's just "what do you want in your coffee," "which shirt do you like for today", something, anything that gives them a bit of control. As a caregiver, you have become the "decider." Giving back control is a huge sacrifice on your part, I know. It makes the process longer, whatever you're doing. You're often met with surprises, like you never knew they wanted oatmeal raisin cookies NOT chocolate chip. Boy, can handing back control cut down on controversy.

45. Watch a sitcom.

Yes, that TV is back on, but make it something funny.

46. Watch a funny movie.

If you have run out of ways to spend time with your loved one, bring a movie or check the guide before you go. Just settle in and enjoy a good time.

47. Wear a red clown nose.
    After I wrote this, Walgreens came up with a promotion to sell Red Noses and raise money for children through having fun! Who can resist a red clown nose? Buy two or three or seven for a bunch a people where your loved one is or goes and take some pics to share with the caregiving world. We would like that!

48. Keep costumes around and dress up
    Or just get dressed up, dress your loved one up. Put on fun clothes or jewelry, or hats. Hats are always great.

49. Do your mom's make-up.
    Okay, if your loved one is Dad or like me, your brother-in-law, make-up isn't the answer, but you could share your Chapstick.

50. Do your mom's hair.
    This is like combing someone's hair, but includes curlers, flat irons, hair spray. Heck, you could color someone's hair. How's that for changing your state?!

51. Do your own makeup with that smoky eye you've been dying to try.
    In numbers 48 and 49 when you get dressed up and/or do Mom's make-up, try that crazy smoky eye on yourself, or Mom. You never know where a cougar might appear.

52. Play Old Maid or Crazy 8's.
    Cards are fun. Who plays cards anymore? Go for it.

53. Play Solitaire.

Maybe you can do this while your loved one goes on and on about the bad food, ugly wallpaper, or their bunions.

54. Meditate.

I've been trying to do this for about three years now. It's not easy, but there's a monk on the Internet that says just concentrate on your breathing. We can all do that. And we can all do that for five minutes. Okay, I'm only up to two minutes, but I'm expanding my horizons!

55. Call a friend

After your friend has calmed you down, hand the phone to your loved one. Let them talk to someone else, too.

56. Ask your dad's advice about a made-up problem.

Because if it's a made up problem, you don't care what the advice is and it won't make you crazy, no matter what they say.

57. Bring in a pet.

It doesn't have to be your pet. In some facilities they have service animals that come to visit, or borrow your neighbor's goldfish.

58. Mani/Pedi.

Do one. Have one. Go get one. Whatever works.

59. Do Laundry.

Yours or theirs, which you are probably doing anyway. How about making it smell really good with a fancy fabric softener? Then fold it together. Who cares if it's done well, it's the doing.

60. Binge watch the Golden Girls, or any other old TV show on Netflix or On Demand. Choose wisely, you don't want to start arguing over the characters' lives. If you choose a program with loads of seasons and episodes you have a built-in distraction or peace maker!

I suspect that even just taking the ten minutes to read this list may have changed your breathing and focus. I hope so. Patience may be the hardest virtue a caregiver has to foster. I'm open to more suggestions!

CHAPTER TEN

CARING FOR THE CAREGIVER...YES, THIS MEANS YOU!

Aunt Mary was a crotchety character, probably why she crocheted 10 hours a day. She thought she was being crotchety but she was mixing up her letters.

I went to her house a few times a week, after Uncle Buddy died because she only had a few nieces and nephews. Her son had sadly passed away before his parents, and her grandchildren lived far away.

Again, I was the designated caregiver because as a stay-at-home mom, I had nothing else to do. Said the stay-at-home mom to no one.

Aunt Mary lived 30 minutes away and required grocery shopping, prescription pick up, supervising her cleaning lady, checking her mail and paying her bills. I took my 3 year-old with me and it was just a few hours out of our day. But after having my Nana for two winters, and discovering I was pregnant. I was starting to feel tired, old, ugly and sad.

My husband saw the downslide and suggested we go to a fancy dinner dance at the club. Yay! A new dress, nails done, hair done, pretty, pretty, pretty me.

I hired a babysitter. I began the day with a fresh outlook. I was excited for the pampering and an evening of dining and dancing. My husband and I love to dance, and it had been a while since we danced the night away.

In the spirit of thinking everyone deserved some fun, I wore that rarely seen sexy thong underwear in the back of my dresser drawer. I kind of hate thongs. They are so darn uncomfortable. But under certain circumstances I must agree. First, the dress looked ever so much better with no panty line. Second, my husband deserved a little fantasy. Which was probably the closest he would get to fantasy because if the evening went the way I thought it would, he would be a bit tipsy, we would both be exhausted from dancing, and we would fall into bed and be snoring a duet within minutes upon our return home.

So off to the ball we went. Cinderella (that's me...code name caregiver) danced with her Prince Charming to every single song they played. Fast, slow, samba, mamba, polka, it didn't matter. If music was playing, we were dancing.

Oh my, so much fun. I made sure to hydrate constantly. I was the designated driver, but I didn't want to wake up to mommyville with a dehydration headache. At some point in time, I decided a trip to the loo was in order. I went in to the ladies' room feeling, hot (as in sexy) confident, happy and just darn groovy.

I go into the stall hike up my dress, go to pull down my panties. Hmmm. I remember just then I'm wearing that darn thong, and gee, I didn't feel the need to grab my own ass the entire night. It is then that I see I have come across a new invention. I am wearing my 'thong' sideways.

Do it all the time now. Too comfortable to go back to tradition.

Every single book on aging parents and caregiving tells you to take care of yourself. Every single caregiver reads that and mutters to herself, "yeah, sure, in my spare time."

I have adopted a new mantra in this arena which you've already heard but I can't say it enough: You must be the healthiest person in the room.

If you are a caregiver, the person you are caring for has health issues. But you don't have to add to your burden by adding health issues of your own. You absolutely must take care of your own physical, mental and spiritual health. There are many ways to do this and some of them can be found in Chapter Eight on "Patience" and here are several more.

Let's talk about why you need to be the healthiest person in the room.

You are battling every day. Your body and mind are in fight or flight mode with insurance companies, doctor's offices, hospital administration, nurses, doctors, physical therapists, occupational therapists, hired caregivers, durable medical equipment people, pharmacists, dietary people, your brother, your spouse, your parent and probably more people than I can mention.

This takes a toll on you, every day for a very long time. You must carve out time for you. You need to understand that this is not selfish, self-centered, self-indulgent or any other 'self' word. It's a necessity. If you don't take the time to exercise, eat right, step away, laugh, have fun, engage in good relationships, go to parties, kiss a baby, have sex, eat chocolate, take a long, hot shower, meditate, or all the other suggestions below, you will become mean, sick, lonely, and perhaps even a caregivee, yourself.

Taking care of oneself does not have to be a gigantic project that you accomplish all in one day. No one does that. You don't even have to take care of yourself every day. I wish that you would. But, I too, have had many days where caregiving was the only thing I did until I fell into bed with exhaustion. That cannot be every single day. If that's what you are doing now, please try and use these suggestions to stave off the guilt, the pain and the exhaustion that comes from caregiving every single day.

1. WALK

Get out there and move. You can walk with your caregivee, if that's possible. Preferably, walk with a friend, or just by yourself. Walk as long as you possibly can. This isn't just exercise. This is a place to go clear your head. Headphones and music are great, too. Choose music that makes you happy, makes you rock out, transports you out of your own head. But this is about walking. I walk with friends or by myself in silence. Never underestimate the joy of silence....and walking.

2. MUSIC

Yes, music and walking go together quite nicely. Listening to music while caregiving can bring a new and refreshing experience to your day. Turn off the television, just for an hour. My brother-in-law was super attached to his TV. He was also deaf in one ear, which we didn't discover until well into his disability. So his TV was on 24/7, literally. He never turned it off. It took me a long time to realize that that banter in my face and all around me when we were trying to discuss his care, or his finances or his children was driving me crazy. If you can, turn off that TV and turn on some nice music for both of you. If not, put on gentle soothing music in your car, I know you're in your car a million times a day.

3. EAT BETTER

There isn't a person on this planet who truly believes that fast food holds the key to good food, a good diet or great nutrition. If you're living on smash and grab food as a caregiver, you need to be more selective. It's not as hard as you think. I once read an amazing book called "Willpower"[1] by Raymond Baumeister and John Tierney. In that book they explain that one of the reasons we run to junk food or sugar, both better known as 'comfort food', when we are stressed is because we have made far too many decisions on that day and our bodies are starving for glucose. Glucose is sugar and we use it up quickly in stressful situations and your body craves to bring itself back to ground zero. That's a ridiculously simplistic explanation from me. If you read this book, and I recommend that you do, it's darn enlightening!

But the point is, you can be aware of your food choices even in stressful times and choose more wisely. I'm not even suggesting a diet. What I am saying is that when you go to McDonald's get a salad or even two salads if you're really hungry. You will feel infinitely better the rest of the day. You will feel better if you take good food with you wherever you go. Buy better food in the grocery store. Buy hummus and carrots and celery. Buy apples and plums and grapes. And then put them in a bag or a lunch cooler and take them with you and eat them. If you scale down on the amount of bad food you are eating and replace it with good food, you are already taking care of the caregiver. You're reducing the chances that YOU have of getting diabetes, high blood pressure, heart ailments. Small incremental changes help you be a better, healthier caregiver. Just do it.

---

[1] Roy F. Baumeister, John Tierney, *Willpower:Discovering the Greatest Human Strength* (The Penguin Press,2011)

4. DRINK WATER

You know you need to do this. You know your caregivee probably needs to do more of this too. Drinking more water is the one thing each and every person can likely do to make their day better. It keeps you hydrated, it staves off hunger, especially when you are actually thirsty and not hungry. It flushes your body of toxins. Water is just a good thing, drink more of it. And share some with your loved one, too. Think of it as a cocktail party!

5. ASK FOR HELP

There's a billion ways to ask for help, I've given you some, lightheartedly and seriously. Outside of the actual words, though, there are places to go and ask for help that you may not even be aware of.

A. Aging and Adult Services

This is the name of the local governmental agencies where I live. It may have a different name where you are, but there is one. Find it. Better yet, ask someone who wants to help to do the research for you. See what services they have available for you and your loved one. The information there is endless and fruitful. They can lead you to Adult Day Care, Respite Care (where your loved one can be cared for overnight while you go out of town), fee sharing for hired caregivers, home health agencies, visiting nurse agencies, programs that may have money for you. This resource has been set up for caregivers and many people don't even know it exists. Google it for your locality, something will pop up. And then call them and use their services.

B. Senior Centers

Depending on your caregiving situation, this is a resource for either your loved one or you. Senior Centers have come a long way. They have classes, support groups, exercise groups, free lunch sometimes. Look into it, it could be a treasure trove you walk by every day.

C. Religious Groups

If you belong to a church or your loved one does, they often have an actual committee that's in place to visit or spend time with sick and elderly parishioners. Your loved one may have been on that committee. His or her church friends may be wondering where your loved one is. Even if it's your church, they may be there to give you a break or come visit with you while you are caregiving.

D. Family

'nuf said….ask.

E. Friends

You may be surprised that your loved one has friends, maybe friends you don't even know about. If it's your spouse, then you likely know those friends. Although, I have quite a few friends at my gym that my husband has never met. And we are always talking about, "hey, where is Ron? He hasn't been at the gym for a few days." I'm pretty sure some of those gym buddies would come and visit me for an hour if my husband needed a little get away. Ask your friends, ask your loved one's friends....it's the very definition of 'friend.' That's why we are lucky enough to have one and be one.

F. Support Groups

There are dozens and dozens of support groups that can be found on Google or in your phone book if you still use one...(we still actually get a phone book in my small town and my mom and her friends do, indeed, use them). The largest employer in my town is the local hospital, and they have many different kinds of support groups as a community service. Look around, they are there for you and for your loved one.

I'm not much of a joiner. Caregivers don't have a lot of extra time for going to meetings, being on the baking committee, or taking field trips. If a caregiver has an extra moment, or hour or half a day, you can be sure most of us will call a friend, take a nap or disappear for as many hours as we can without being detected, all in the name of sanity.

I find that support and support groups for caregivers probably look different from those same groups for shared illness, grief or other struggles. That's why the internet is a godsend to caregivers. It is much easier to get online for a few minutes, or even an hour to find answers, comfort, or someone else who is really, in real time going through the same issues you are as a caregiver.

There are dozens, if not hundreds of online support groups for caregivers. I'm listing a few here as I have engaged in these and find them filled with caring people with good advice and good monitors.

They are not snarky, judgmental places. People here are in the trenches just like you and have some great answers, and you may have great answers for them as well.

I am not in any way opposed to real life support groups. I believe that if a caregiver can find the time and resources to get to a place where she can meet with real live people, she should hop on that ASAP. And there are such places as I mentioned above. If your loved one is in a facility of any kind, there is surely a support group there. If there isn't and you would like to start one that would be wonderful. I'm sure the staff would welcome that kind of commitment to the caregivers who visit with their loved ones.

I often found myself in the dining room, the solarium or even the lobby of the many assisted living facilities or nursing homes I've been attached to, falling into conversation with a fellow caregiver about one thing or another and it became a five-minute support group.

Support groups, whether they are in person or online fall well within the parameters of a caregiver taking care of herself/himself. In a brief and unscientific survey that I constructed of those who read my blog or follow me on Facebook and are well aware of my caregiving journey, support for the caregiver was a need that every single person noted.

Caregivers do not take support lightly, in fact, we love support. I don't want to confuse getting support through support groups with getting help in our actual day-to-day caregiving. I would highly recommend that you take a look at some of these online support groups to see if there's anything there for you, either as a taker or a giver. Caregivers, including you, are a wealth of knowledge. We encounter crazy problems and situations every day that somehow seem to be the "first time anyone has ever seen this." Your experience and resolutions could be the difference between an hour on the phone or two days tracking down vital information to some other overwhelmed and bewildered caregiver. Plus, it feels just as good to give as it does to receive in caregiving support.

So here are my online support group suggestions, if you have anything to add please go to my website www.cathysikorski.com to the contact page and let me know, I will add it to my Resources tab to share with everyone else.

Online Support Groups:

1. On AgingCare.com Support Forum

   https://www.agingcare.com/Caregiver-Forum

2. Family Caregiver Alliance

   https://www.caregiver.org/support-groups

3. Caring.com

   https://www.caring.com/support-groups

CHAPTER ELEVEN

HOW TO MAKE WORK, WORK FOR YOU.

There's a tendency in corporate life to see caregivers as a drain on the economy in general and on the company, specifically. The interesting thing is that study after study has shown that by addressing the *fact of caregivers* in your workforce, a company actually can make business better.

1. START THE CONVERSATION

You just have to talk. If you're the boss and the employer or if you're the caregiver. This is a two-way street that requires communication.

This summer I binge watched the Gilmore Girls with my grown daughter. Episode after episode we would just look at each other and say: "If only they would talk to each other, they could resolve that problem." That is the first downfall of caregivers in the work place.

Employers have claimed for years that they are unaware of employees dealing with caregiving issues. Employees admittedly have failed to tell their employers that they are dealing with caregiving issues.

The conversation has to begin.

Employees have to be honest about the issues they are dealing with. They have to stop hiding the phone calls, taking "long lunches" that are actually runs to the nursing home, doctor's office, hairdresser or pharmacy for your caregivee. Employees need to be able to work around their caregiving issues. The key here being work. Employees really do want to work. They don't want to take care of their moms or dads, at least not in the sense that instead of being productive at work, they would rather be dealing with health issues, nurses, doctors, hospitals or insurance companies. Most of us would rather be at our office doing what we are being paid to do without interruption.

Yes, it's like having small children or even teenagers. But it's worse in many ways. Children go to daycare, they go to school, they grow up and leave us with an empty nest. This is not the life of the caregiver. It does not get better, it only gets worse. This is the way of the world. The statistics are grim in that regard. There are more people getting old and less people around to care for them. What that means is that working life and caregiving life will have to come to a compromise position. Employers and employees will need to figure out a way to do this and do it well. It can be done. Many major employers have banded together to look at this issue and see how employers and employees can make this work for everyone involved. We have made great progress in the world of childcare, and caregiving is the next step. Employed caregivers of adults need to stop believing they are the ugly step-sisters of employed caregivers of children.

Let the games begin.

You, as an employee must confess. And you, as an employer, must give your employees the safe space to hear what's going on in their lives. That's the big catch. Employees don't tell employers their troubles, especially if it will be seen as a detriment to their work, their progress, or their commitment to the job. The only way an employer can help is if they know they need to help. Employers need to be open to helping. The perception is that an employer is not open to helping, that an employer does not even *want* to know that help is required. Research seems to indicate otherwise. Employers are implementing small and large programs that indicate employers do want to know and they want to help caregivers.

Employers must make it known that help is on the way. Caregivers need to know that there are benefits to help caregivers. But more importantly, caregivers need to know that they can have a simple conversation with their supervisor, manager or HR person telling them that they are steeped in caregiving and need some consideration. Until this conversation is seen as a possibility for resolution and not an invitation to getting demoted or fired, the conversation will never begin.

Once the conversation is allowed by employers, once employees feel safe to have this conversation, then matters can move forward for both parties.

2. GIVE AND TAKE

Both employers and employees are going to need to give and take here. It is astounding that there are many corporate employee benefits for caregivers that go unnoticed and unused. Many corporations have caregiving benefits in place far beyond the minimum requirements of the Family and Medical Leave Act (FMLA). This is the law that was enacted in 1993 (which gives certain covered employees of certain employers) granting 12 weeks of unpaid leave for medical necessity of the employee or certain members of the employees' family. That's a lot of "certains". If you work for an employer who has over 50 employees where you work, you are likely covered for FMLA after one year of employment.

Outside of the FMLA, the benefits that are available to you as an employee are specific to your company. But they are often there. Go look for them. Look in your handbook, talk to your HR person, ask the lady at the desk next to you who has been telling you for years about her mother's complaints from her assisted living facility.

Your employer may have such benefits as:

a. Geriatric Care Managers

b. Flex time

c. Job sharing

d. Adult Day Care connections

e. Reduced Cost for Adult Day Care

f. Reduced Cost for In-Home Care

g. Reduced Cost for Legal Consultation and Fees

h. Long-term Care Insurance at no cost or reduced cost

i. Long term Care Insurance for your parents

j. Nursing consultations through your Employee Health Insurance

k. Geriatric Planning through your health insurance

These are just some of the benefits that are often un-sung and are sitting right at the doorstep of your job.

Many employers, especially large corporations, have begun to recognize the plight of the caregiver who tries to remain a good employee and have implemented some of these programs. Just ask.

As to employers, I might suggest you look into these types of programs. Many of them are available through your Employee Health Insurance. You may not even know of the benefits available to your employees, that you, as a great employer are already providing!

Additionally, I'd like to direct you to this super cool website provided by MetLife for employers:

http://www.eldercarecalculator.org/

In seconds it will literally do the calculation for you as to how much money you may be losing by not implementing meaningful programs like flex time, job sharing and telecommuting. That nincompoop over at Yahoo, who took away all telecommuting from the entire company has been proven wrong. Studies continue to show…even in China….that working at home can be more productive, less costly and a benefit to employer and employee alike.

The point here is that for both you as an employee and you as an employer looking at the reality of increased caregiving responsibilities in today's world, a working life can work for both of you and be successful.

CHAPTER TWELVE

AIN'T NO SHAME IN LAUGHING

The top ten ways you know you may be 'One of Us!'

1. *When you know Medicare's phone number and website without Googling....Yep, You're One of Us!*

2. *When your search for an Assisted Living Community for your mom starts to look like a nice vacation spot for you and your spouse....Yep, You're One of Us!*

3. *When you cancel your dentist appointment to attend Ice Cream Social Wednesday at your dad's nursing home, because you want the ice cream....Yep, You're One of Us!*

4. *When you know your parents' Medicare number, AARP number, United Healthcare number but not your own cell phone number...Yep, You're One of Us!*

5. *When you feel the need to correct WebMD about all the missed additional symptoms of a urinary tract infection....Yep, You're One of Us!*

6. *When your iPhone calendar has words on it like 'catheters', 'hearing aid', 'urologist', or 'dentures'.....Yep, You're One of Us!*

7. *When going to the Emergency Room is like Cheers where they know your first name and how you take your coffee..... Yep, You're One of Us!*

8. *When you took the black Sharpie to your husband's underwear to mark it for the wash instead of your mom's for the nursing home.....Yep, You're One of Us!*

9. *When you've had more knock-down, drag-out fights with insurance companies, hospitals and doctor's office than Muhammad Ali.....Yep, You're One of Us!*

10. *When everyone around you thinks you are speaking in tongues you are constantly saying, PT, OT, UTI, or DME....Yep, You're One of Us!*

I entered the world of caregiving by accident over 25 years ago and never left. Early on, I realized a sense of humor might be a helpful tool. I would use laughter to entertain myself if no one else was interested in laughing at my predicament. And then just a few short years ago, I began a blog called. "You Just have to Laugh.... Where caregiving is comedy."

That blog was a way for me to vent my daily frustrations, anger issues, impatience, incredulity and anything else that was driving me crazy that day, week, month or year of caregiving. I had already written *"Showering with Nana: Confessions of a Serial (killer) Caregiver."* My book was published as I was writing my blog. I had moved so far beyond my first experience taking care of my Nana and my toddler, as a member of the Sandwich Generation, which was the topic of that book. I realized that the humor I found in that first experience was deeply entrenched in all my caregiving experience. It occurred to me that the universal caregiver was steeped in universal craziness and humor if you just looked at it the right way.

While I love to write humor, and I know that when I'm dealing with an unreasonable person from Medicare, Social Security, any Medigap Insurance Company, the pharmacist, a doctor's office, a billing office, Comcast the uber internet and tv provider, a bank, a hospital, or any of the other dozens of people we meet and talk to as caregivers, I am likely *eventually* going to look back on this frustrating experience and laugh and definitely see the humor in it. So why not start the laughing now?

I'm fairly certain this, too is a universal caregivers' experience.

That is why I'm committed to spreading the joy of laughter and humor throughout the caregiving world. I would love for you all to become followers of my blog at www.cathysikorski.com. I also want to share with you the many general and specific ways to bring humor into your life as a caregiver, caregivee, or just one who is smart enough to be reading this book as a look towards the future.

1. READ FUNNY BOOKS

Every well-known comedian has a book out there. There's a comedy section in every major book store. I love independent book sellers, go there and ask for the comedy section. If you can't get out of the house because of caregiving. Go online. Amazon abounds with comedic books. If you don't want to spend money, call your local library. My library has books online, you can sign up and get books into your cellphone or tablet or computer. Do it. It's worth the time and money…and if it's your public library, it's free.

2. WATCH FUNNY TV AND YOUTUBE VIDEOS

If you have a computer find your funny on YouTube. There's something for everyone. If you don't have access to a computer or smartphone, watch comedy on TV. Watch sitcoms, or funny movies, or cartoons, whatever makes you laugh. My family loves a show called "Whose Line Is It Anyway?" It's an improvisational comedy show on TV and it just never fails to get all of us laughing hard and loudly. Find whatever that is that works for you.

3. LISTEN TO COMEDIANS

Sirius radio has several comedy channels, Comedy Central, Raw Dog, Comedy. Find the station you like and keep it on speed dial. Comedians put out albums all the time. If you listen to music on your phone with headphones, change it up and find some comedy. There's a billion kinds of comedy to choose from. You will not be able to say there's nothing you like. There's comedy out there for everyone. Put in a few minutes and find it.

4. GO TO LIVE SHOWS

I know, you're a caregiver. Getting away is not easy. If that's true for you, all these other options apply and can rev up your laugh meter. If you are the kind of caregiver who can go out, go out and get laughing. There are comedy clubs, comedy charity events, amusing theater. Go. Getting out is good. Getting out and laughing is better.

5. GO TO THE MOVIES...THE FUNNY ONES

Sometimes this can be more of a challenge to your day than caregiving. Yes, a good hilarious movie is hard to find. But try. It's so worth it. Sometimes lower your standards....you might be surprised. And go, go to the movies, not watch one at home. You should watch them at home, as much as you can, but if you have the opportunity to get out you should. It's better that way.

6. **READ FUNNY THINGS ON THE INTERNET**
Rather than waiting for someone to post something hilarious on Facebook, because you have to wade through the other stuff that will make you insane, find some good comedy websites for reading. One of my favorites is www.HumorOutcasts.com. Full disclosure here, I am a writer on that website. But there are over 100 writers who contribute to that website, so you can find many other funny, charming and hilarious things to tickle your funny bone.

Thank you from the bottom of my heart for taking this caregiving journey with me. If you go to my website, you will find that I have entered many of the great resources I have found to be helpful along the way. Feel free to contact me there with any information you may have that is helpful to you or other caregivers. The more we share the wealth, the more we lessen the burden. My love to all you hard-working caregivers. You're the best!

Cathy Sikorski

ACKNOWLEDGMENTS

I continue to be blessed and surrounded by people of great talent who are always so kind and willing to give of their gifts.

Thanks to my beta readers and trusted colleagues who gave great suggestions for making this work better, Terri Newmyer, Tina Dahms and Jean Dames.

To my friends, Sally and John Hersh who so generously shared their beach house during the off season to give me time and seclusion to work through this project. And to John Sikorski, Tom and Terri Newmyer, and Lisa Weil who broke up the seclusion so I could keep going.

To my generous and smart blog readers who kindly took a Survey Monkey questionnaire to help decide what's important to adult children, aging parents and caregivers. And to those same blog readers who constantly shore me up with their supportive comments on my weekly blog, where I just try to keep all of us laughing.

To Stuart Horwitz, whose books, *Book Architecture* and *Finish Your Book in Three Drafts: How to Write a Book, Revise a Book and Complete A Book While You Still Love It,* were invaluable in aiding the process of structuring this work. Not to mention Stuart's kind emails in answer to all my questions concerning his methods.

To Donna Cavanagh, my Publisher Extraordinaire who has great faith in me when I'm not so sure she should, who promotes my books and all her authors with gusto and dedication that is a rare gift in publishing today, and who I am so lucky to call my friend and literary partner.

To my husband, John, my daughter Rachel and my new son-in-law, Brendan, and my daughter Margot, all of whom keep me grounded but willingly act as my cheerleaders whenever I need it. And to my Mom, who still lets me pretend I'm caregiving for her, when it's really her doing it for me.